W9-AXH-839

Cambridge

1 (overleaf) King's College Chapel: the Organ (1688) and the Main Vault (John Wastell, Master Mason, 1512-15)

CAMBRIDGE

F. A. Reeve

With photographs by
Eric de Maré

B. T. BATSFORD LTD
London

First published 1964

© F. A. Reeve, 1964

MADE AND PRINTED IN GREAT BRITAIN BY
WILLIAM CLOWES AND SONS LTD, LONDON AND BECCLES
for the publishers B. T. BATSFORD LTD
4 FITZHARDINGE STREET, PORTMAN SQUARE, LONDON W.1

CONTENTS

ACKNOWLEDGMENT

The illustration on the jacket is of the Gatehouse of St. John's College and is reproduced from a colour transparency by Eric de Maré.

The author and publishers would like to thank the Syndics of the Cambridge University Press for their permission to reproduce a detail from Hamond's map of Cambridge of 1592 which appears on Page 63.

THE ILLUSTRATIONS

Introduction

IS CAMBRIDGE the only true university town still to be found in Great Britain? The claim is often made, though perhaps it exaggerates the recent changes at Oxford, and overlooks Durham and St. Andrews. A 'true university town' is primarily a town where the academic buildings—the colleges, laboratories and libraries—are intermingled with residential and commercial property to present a varied townscape, something quite unlike the more modern foundations where the university buildings form a distinct group apart from, and sometimes outside the city. In Cambridge, as in Oxford, one may cross a noisy street, pass through an imposing or a humble gateway, and enter a succession of peaceful courts. One can sense a complete contrast between the streets, with their mixture of academic and commercial buildings, and the college courts. The visitor can take a few steps and pass from the twentieth century into the Middle Ages.

There are some who maintain that Cambridge is no longer a true university town, that the advent of chain-stores and modern blocks of commercial buildings that have replaced small units of varying size and height have already ruined its character. One must admit that much has already been lost, but incomparable glories still remain. Nothing can alter the splendour of the Backs, the colleges that succeed one another along the banks of the river, with their spacious and still secluded grounds, impeccable lawns and beautiful flowers. Queen's Road, when first I knew it, was a quiet country lane with only a few bicycles, carriages or carts. Now the flow of cars and lorries is unceasing, but one can still pause to look at one of the finest views in the world— Clare College, King's College Chapel, and Gibbs' Building, rising beyond the great expanse of lawn.

Apart from the college and university buildings, the Cambridge street architecture is not impressive, not as outstanding as at Chester, Stratford or York. But a few remarkable streets remain. King's Parade, one of the best urban vistas in the country, the town buildings of differing heights, frontages and materials on one side providing a striking contrast to the more important academic structures opposite. In Trinity Street and St. John's Street only a few of the individual buildings are of outstanding merit, yet the whole effect is most pleasing. There is great variety—a half-timber and plaster Elizabethan building, a Georgian structure of mellow red brick, among other small and diverse units, then the ancient dull brick of St. John's and the small garden on the site of the demolished All Saints. In Magdalene Street, old and picturesque houses faced with painted plaster and with a diverse roof-line remain practically unchanged externally.

The college and the university buildings do not dominate the streets as in Oxford, and until the nineteenth century the colleges were small-scale, many only partially visible behind high walls, or almost completely masked by town buildings. The academic buildings in Oxford are more coherent and often of a more ambitious design; Cambridge is more informal, more modest. A large modern block replacing a row of small-unit properties can completely alter the scale of a two-storey college, and Christ's College appears to have become much smaller and less significant since the big new Prudential House was built almost beside it.

There is little industry, so the buildings remain remarkably clean. The needs of the University largely dictated what is made in Cambridge —the important Pye enterprise began when W. G. Pye, appointed in 1892 to make scientific apparatus at the Cavendish Laboratory, decided to open his own workshop. Undergraduates asked the keeper of the University racquets courts to supply them with equipment, so H. J. Gray began to manufacture it. The founder of Marshall's garage was caterer to the Pitt Club; when members began to acquire cars, he opened a garage nearby to house and service them. In more recent times, many modest privately-financed research establishments founded by Cambridge scientists have become important firms. Printing, book-selling and bookbinding firms developed to fulfil academic needs, and hundreds of building workers are at any time erecting new constructions or are engaged on the never-ending task of renovating ancient colleges.

The reader may be unfamiliar with a few words which will often be used. A 'Combination Room' is a comfortably-furnished lounge for the senior members of a college, and at a 'Buttery' the under-graduates can obtain groceries. 'Screens' are wooden partitions on both sides of a passage-way between dining-halls and kitchens, and on which notices are displayed. The word 'Fellow', a translation of the Latin '*socius*', originally meant students who received free board and lodging, but a Fellow is now a man who has taken his degree and has been elected to a fellowship; he may be engaged in teaching, research or administration, and he receives a 'dividend' or share of the college revenues. A 'Scholar' is a man who sat for a college examination before he came into residence, and was awarded a scholarship.

Most visitors come to Cambridge to see the colleges, to admire beautiful buildings and the incomparable 'Backs'. To appreciate them fully, one should know something of their history, of the mode of life of those who have lived in them through the centuries, and of the dons and undergraduates who inhabit them today. We will accordingly first consider how the University and the city evolved, then how the students work and play, before we finally saunter through courts and grounds.

I

The Past

THE EARLY MIDDLE AGES 1

*Early settlements. The coming of the first scholars and friars.
The thirteenth-century town*

ALTHOUGH OXFORD had scholars at an earlier date, it is not such an ancient city. Cambridge was an important place long before the first scholars arrived early in the thirteenth century. There was habitable ground on both sides of the river at a point where it could be crossed, and high ground on the left bank facilitated the defence of the river crossing. This favourable site attracted very early settlements, and from prehistoric times a network of tracks provided lines of communication to the Norfolk coast and to the Thames. The heavy clay soil to the west was densely forested, there were more forests to the south, and to the north stretched the undrained Fens. In between ran a narrow belt of pasture and chalk downs, about five miles wide at its narrowest point, and travellers between the country of the East Angles and ancient Mercia (now the Midlands), could only cross the river at Cambridge. Both Oxford and Cambridge were frontier towns, important river-crossings and road junctions.

A Roman settlement of houses built of wood and clay, with thatched roofs, occupied about 28 acres on Castle Hill. There were causeways on both sides of a ford, and later, a bridge; in 1823 the east causeway of wooden beams on piles was discovered 14 feet below the present street level. Akeman Street, branching from Ermine Street, entered the Roman town and continued to the Isle of Ely, and the road from the south-east to Godmanchester crossed the river near the present Great Bridge. In Roman and Saxon times there was no direct road between Cambridge and London; travellers had to go through Royston, Dunstable and St. Albans.

'Anglo-Saxon' invaders, who replaced the Romanised Britons during the Pagan period, occupied the area on the right bank between the churches of Great St. Mary's and St. Bene't's. The Danes wintered in Cambridge in 875, and the town was burnt in 1010, but was no doubt quickly rebuilt. A market was well established before the Norman Conquest, and there were probably many houses near the market place. By means of the river, the town was in direct communication with the Continent, and there were wharves near the present site of St. Clement's church. Situated on almost the only line of communication between East Anglia and the rest of England, Cambridge became an important centre of trade, and the wealth of the merchants facilitated the building of St. Bene't's church in about 1025.

After the Conquest, King William destroyed 27 houses to erect a castle, probably built of wood. From this stronghold, Sheriff Picot made heavy demands upon the townsfolk, and the Chronicle of Ely written by a twelfth-century monk described him as 'a hungry lion, a ravening wolf, a filthy hog'. In 1092, at the request of his devout wife, Picot established a church dedicated to St. Giles near the castle, with accommodation for six canons. His successor, Pain Peverel, removed them in 1112 to a site outside the town at Barnwell, and established a house for 30 Augustinian canons. Barnwell Priory, said to have had a church 200 feet long, profoundly influenced life in Cambridge during the Middle Ages.

About 20 years later, a house of Benedictine nuns was established in what is now Jesus Lane. The nuns of St. Radegund built a large church which survives in part as the beautiful Chapel of Jesus College. The nunnery was also outside the town, and villages grew up around both of these religious foundations. At about the same time, the Hospital of St. Mary Magdalene for lepers was established to the east of the town, and its little chapel still stands beside the Newmarket Road. King John granted the Hospital a fair, the celebrated Sturbridge Fair, which in Elizabethan times became the largest and most famous in Great Britain.

The first charter, granted by Henry I, recognised the borough court and gave the town a monopoly of the river trade. Ships were forbidden to discharge at any other hythe in the shire. Two charters of King John (1201 and 1207) consolidated the position of the town as a corporation. The second granted the town to the burgesses in fee farm, and made them independent of the Sheriff in financial matters.

The burgesses were authorised to appoint their own reeve, and later writs mention bailiffs. Four bailiffs, one each for the Bridge, Market, High and Mill Wards, were elected annually, and a Mayor is first mentioned in 1231. In 1224 Henry III granted to the burgesses the house of Benjamin the Jew, and it later became the Town Hall. Two charters of 1227 confirmed those of John, and from 1256 the town was no longer responsible to the Sheriff in administrative matters. All the soil of the town and the meadows, pastures, mills, waters and pools belonged to the town. Control of the river included fishing rights, and until the days of Charles II the Mayor and aldermen went 'a-fishing according to custom'. Merchants built hythes beside the river on land rented from the town.

A guild of thegns, a society of country gentlemen, was established in the eleventh century for their mutual protection and to serve as a burial club, and by the thirteenth century there were many parish guilds with religious and social aims, which provided pensions for members in need, masses for the dead, and lights for church services.

There were serious disturbances in Oxford in 1209, and most of the masters and scholars left the town. Some went to Reading, others to Cambridge. It is probable that they chose Cambridge because it was an important town, with good communications, and already had a type of grammar school. The majority of the migrants returned to Oxford five years later, but some of the masters and students remained to lay the foundations of the University of Cambridge.

The mediaeval students were only 14 or 15 years old when they entered the University, the masters often only 21. Some were extremely poor, and frequently had to beg. Various benefactors founded chests from which money could be borrowed by those who could deposit a suitable security. At first the scholars lodged in private houses or inns, but complaints of over-charging led to the establishment of a number of hostels or lodging-houses controlled by a master. The students were ill-disciplined and high-spirited, and there were frequent affrays with the townsmen.

In about 1225, when Franciscan Friars arrived in Cambridge, some teachers were lecturing regularly, and a few hostels had probably been established. The townsfolk allowed the Friars to occupy half of the house of Benjamin the Jew, and here they remained for 40 years; the other part was used as a gaol. A document of 1226 mentions a Chancellor of the University. Chancellors were always resident, and performed many of the functions of the Vice-Chancellor today. Disturbances in the University of Paris in 1229 led Henry III to invite foreign students to come to England, and some no doubt arrived in Cambridge. The landlords and hostel-keepers raised rents, and there were frequent disputes between them and the students. The University authorities found it difficult to maintain order, and in 1231 the King had to intervene. He issued four writs intended to organise the University more efficiently and to control the students. They decreed that 'troublesome and rebellious clerks' should be reported by the Chancellor and Masters to the Bishop of Ely; he would inform the Sheriff, who was required to detain them, not in the town gaol but in the castle, and must heed the advice of the University authorities when he inflicted punishments. The King decreed that all clerks must be under the tuition of a Master, and that the rents of their lodgings should be assessed by two Masters and two townsmen called 'Taxors'. These officials continued to act until 1856. In 1242 the Chancellor obtained power to report offending students direct to the Sheriff.

The presence of several Orders of mendicant friars had a great influence on the growth of the University. By 1240 the Franciscans numbered 20–25, and they had secured the whole of the house of Benjamin the Jew. The Dominicans, the Black or Preaching Friars, who gave their name to Preacher's Street (now St. Andrew's Street), were building their house on the site of Emmanuel in 1238. Cambridge was one of the four Visitations into which the Dominican Province in England was divided, and the priory was intended for 70 friars.

In 1249 the Carmelites, after a brief sojourn in Chesterton, moved to Newnham and built a church, cloister, dormitory and other

2 *Corpus Christi College: the Fourteenth-century Old Cou*
3 *Queens' College: the President's Gallery (c. 154(*

apartments, on a site of about three acres. When they found that winter floods often made it impossible to go to the town to buy food, or for scholars to come to them, they moved in 1292 to Milne Street, and their grounds eventually extended from what is now the first court of Queens' to the neighbourhood of King's Chapel. The north wall of their church still exists as the boundary between King's and Queens'. The Friars of the Sack were welcomed in 1258, and gifts from the townspeople, and especially from the Le Rus family, enabled them to obtain premises near the church of St. Peter in Trumpington Road. They were prominent in the University until they were suppressed in 1307. The Franciscans originally settled in Cambridge to assist the needy and to obtain recruits for their Order. By 1260 they had a well-established system for training teachers at each convent, and a majority of the friars at Cambridge had been sent there to study.

There were constant feuds, not only between the students and the townsmen, but also between scholars from the north and those from the south. In 1261, townsfolk took part in a serious affray between the rival groups, houses were raided, and University records burnt. The King intervened and referred the affair to three justices; 16 townsmen were executed, and some southern scholars received a royal pardon. After this serious disturbance, some students migrated to Northampton, but in 1265 the King forbade them to continue to reside there. Prince Edward attempted to settle town and gown disputes in 1270, and decreed that both clerks and laymen should try to keep the peace and must take an annual oath to preserve the privileges of the University. Six years later, the Bishop of Ely ruled that although the clergy of the town churches came under the jurisdiction of the archdeacon, priests who came to Cambridge to study were answerable to the Chancellor.

Almost all of the town was enclosed by the King's Ditch, which left the river at the bottom of Mill Lane, ran across the site of the New Museums, crossed St. Andrew's Street just north-west of Christ's, passed through the grounds of Sidney Sussex, and rejoined the river near the electricity works. Even this small area was not completely built upon in early mediaeval times. There were houses between the High Street (now King's Parade and Trinity Street), and Conduit

King's College Chapel and the Fellows' Building (Gibbs, 1723-9)
Clare College (1638-1715)

Street (now Sidney Street), but the ground between the parishes of St. Sepulchre and All Saints, and the houses of St. Clement's parish near the bridge, was swampy. When a townsman founded the Hospital of St. John in about 1200, it was built on artificially raised ground at the northern end of the High Street.

A fourth group of houses stood between the west side of the High Street and the river. Milne Street was an important thoroughfare parallel with the High Street; it ran from the mills near Queens' to the site of the Queen's Gate of Trinity, where it turned east to join the High Street. Parts of Milne Street still exist as Queens' Lane and Trinity Hall Lane. From Milne Street and the northern part of the High Street, several lanes led to the riverside hythes, and the neighbourhood was served by the church of St. John Zachery. The Jews in Cambridge settled mainly between All Saints', opposite St. John's College, and the Round Church, and after they were expelled in 1275, this area was for long called the Old Jewry.

Houses were built of timber and thatch, but Hervey fitz Eustace, an important man between 1200 and 1240, and the earliest Mayor whose name is known, owned a stone manor-house built towards the end of the twelfth century. This house is called, for unknown reasons, the School of Pythagoras; it still stands behind Northampton Street, and is the oldest secular building in the city. The descendants of Hervey fitz Eustace became impoverished, and sold the property to Merton College, Oxford, in 1270–1. In 1279 it was described as 'the stone house of the scholars of Merton'. From the fifteenth until the nineteenth century it was leased to farmers who enlarged the adjoining buildings and used the original stone house as a granary, and from 1872–4 the extensions, named Merton Hall, accommodated the foundation for women students that was to become Newnham College.

The townsmen became responsible for enforcing order in 1268, and the Mayor and bailiffs were assisted by two aldermen, four senior burgesses, and two sworn men from each parish. Scholars who attacked laymen were tried by the Chancellor. In 1270 the town and the University assumed joint responsibility for the maintenance of the peace, and appointed 10 burgesses and 10 scholars annually at a meeting summoned by the Vice-Chancellor, called the Black Assembly because on these occasions he wore a black robe. These meetings were resented by the townsmen, since they emphasised the subordination of the town to the University.

The Barons, after their defeat at Evesham in 1265, made a stand in the Isle of Ely, and in the following year plundered the surrounding country. Henry III brought an army to Cambridge, made the King's Ditch a more formidable obstacle, and erected gates where it was crossed by the Trumpington Road and what is now St. Andrew's Street. The Earl of Gloucester captured London, the King withdrew his troops, and the Islanders attacked the town and burnt the gates. The King's Ditch can never have been a very effective defence, and for centuries it was a depository for all manner of refuse. There were complaints that privies were built over it, and owing to the very slight natural fall of the water, little of the filth was carried away. In 1268 the King ordered the Ditch to be cleansed, because 'what was meant for fortifying had become a great annoying'.

The Great Bridge, the only one in England to have given its name to a county, was also a source of dissension. The Sheriff, to whom county landowners had to pay pontage rents, was responsible for its maintenance, but after it had been damaged by floods in 1273, he increased the tax and promised to build a new bridge of stone, but only repaired it with timber. The keeper of the castle prison took away planks by night, and by 1279 the bridge was so unsafe that carts fell into the river. The Sheriff then obtained more money by making people pay to be ferried across. In later times, the county taxpayers constantly protested that they were obliged to pay for the upkeep of the bridge, although it principally benefited the town. When a new stone bridge was erected in 1754, the cost was met by public subscription, and the present iron bridge constructed in 1823 was also mainly financed by private contributions.

In 1279 there were still no colleges, but 17 churches, excluding those of the religious houses, 76 shops or stalls, and 535 messuages. The castle was strengthened in the late twelfth and early in the thirteenth century, but it was in a dilapidated state when, between 1286–96, Edward I made it an efficient stronghold and spent two nights there in 1293. Walls and towers, a hall, chambers and a gatehouse were constructed, but it was never attacked and served mainly as a prison. Henry VI allowed stone to be removed from it for the building of King's, and in later years it was used as a quarry during the building of Sawston Hall, Emmanuel, and Magdalene. By 1606, only the gatehouse survived. From 1295 Cambridge sent two representatives to Parliament, who until 1625 were elected by a small number of burgesses, usually only eight.

THE EARLY MIDDLE AGES 2

The mediaeval University and the first colleges, Peterhouse, Michaelhouse, King's Hall and University Hall

The paramount official of the University was the Chancellor, and for about 300 years he was elected annually. He had his own court for causes involving students, whom he could imprison, expel or excommunicate. Next in importance were the two Proctors, elected annually from among the Regent Masters, i.e. men who taught and lectured. They controlled the finances of the University and the sale of foodstuffs, and could punish students who broke University regulations. Two Esquire Bedells were obliged to attend all University ceremonies and disputations, and two Taxors were elected annually to fix, with two townsmen, the rents of houses occupied by scholars, and to supervise the markets. Non-Regent Masters were graduates concerned with their own hostel or religious house. Statutes had to be approved by a majority of both Regents and Non-Regents.

Most of the students knew little beyond reading, writing and some Latin when they entered the University. The course of study lasted for seven years, although a majority did not stay for so long. It consisted of the *Trivium* (Grammar, Rhetoric and Logic), leading to the B.A. Degree after four years, and the *Quadrivium* (Arithmetic, Geometry, Astronomy, Music). Those who took the grammar course under the supervision of a Master of Glomery aspired only to be schoolmasters. For a degree in theology it was necessary to study for 16 or 17 years.

In the early years of the University the only books possessed by lecturers were in manuscript. After the lecturer had read from his MS he would propose a question and require his students to argue for and against it. Writing materials were scarce and expensive, so examinations consisted of Disputations. Latin was the language of the Church and the learned, and every mediaeval student had to be able to write and converse in that language. Candidates for degrees had to state some proposition which they were willing to defend, and an M.A. known as the Prevaricator would attack the students' propositions. A senior graduate called the Moderator presided over the Disputations.

The University occupied ordinary dwelling-houses and did not erect any schools for teaching or for administrative purposes until about 200 years after the arrival of the first scholars. In 1278 it owned three houses probably used for teaching, and at about the same time another house called the Arts School. A dwelling opposite Great St. Mary's church in which theology, canon and civil law was taught was rented in 1309. A large hall was needed for certain ceremonies, and Great St. Mary's became the University Church from a very early time. There is no record of any formal agreement between the University and the parishioners, but in later years the University claimed that it had a right to use it. Sermons were preached by eminent churchmen, and the University met in it to transact its administrative affairs.

In 1275, for instance, there was a Congregation to make rules for the better discipline of the scholars. The town authorities also used this church, and there were sometimes joint meetings. In mediaeval times the naves of churches had no seating except a few movable benches, and they were used for many purposes for which secular halls are used today. Goods were bought and sold in parish churches, and in 1346 the town authorities forbade this. A fire engine was kept in one of the chapels of Great St. Mary's in the eighteenth century. Two important annual ceremonies were held in this church, the *Comitia Priora*, an examination for the B.A. which began on Ash Wednesday, and the *Comitia Maxima*, later called the Commencement, for M.A. candidates, and held at the beginning of July. St. Bene't's and the churches of the friars were also sometimes used for assemblies.

The religious houses attracted many needy students and there were complaints that boys were being induced to enrol when they were still too young to realise the full consequences of their action. Walter de Merton's college at Oxford, in 1264 the first English foundation, expressly excluded all members of the religious orders.

The first Cambridge college was established at a time when there were serious conflicts with the townsmen, and its founder was following Walter de Merton's example of 20 years earlier. In the year 1280, Edward I allowed Hugh de Balsham, Bishop of Ely, to introduce some scholars into the Hospital of St. John. He was a Benedictine, and by placing secular students with the friars he endeavoured to combine the two elements in the University. The brethren and the scholars, however, could not live together harmoniously, and in 1284 the Bishop removed the students to two hostels just outside the Trumpington Gate, between St. Peter's church and the property of the Friars of the Sack, and assigned to them the tithes of the church. When he died two years later, he left 300 marks to the college, and with this sum they bought land and erected a fine Hall, of which parts still survive. For the next 130 years the scholars lodged in houses already on the site, since after the Hall had been put up, lack of funds prevented any additional buildings. In 1307, when the Friars of the Sack had been dissolved, the college obtained their land and house to the south. The scholars were secular, and the endowment was independent of any religious house. In common with all the early colleges, the neighbouring parish church served for their devotions.

Hugh de Balsham's successor at Ely gave Peterhouse its first code of statutes, modelled on that of Merton; it made provision for a Master and 14 perpetual Fellows 'studiously engaged in the pursuit of literature' and 'so far as human frailty admit, he be honourable, chaste, peaceable, humble, and modest'. One of the statutes ordained that 'the Master and all and each of the scholars of our house shall adopt the clerical dress and tonsure . . . and not allow their beard or their hair to grow contrary to canonical prohibition, nor wear rings upon their fingers for their own vain glory and boasting. . . .'

The real meaning of the word 'college' is a society of people, not the building they inhabit. The buildings were called the *domus* (house) or *aula* (hall). Colleges were created and endowed by private benefactors to provide accommodation and a small stipend for scholars unable to remain at the University without assistance. It should be noted that they were intended for teachers, not for students, and the latter were not admitted until well into the sixteenth century. Students were then allowed to enter on payment of an annual rent or 'pension'. The early colleges consisted only of chambers, a hall and a kitchen, and a long time elapsed before courts were erected to a definite plan, and provision made for a chapel, library, Master's lodge, and the stately gateways which are such a feature of collegiate architecture in Cambridge. Oxford and Cambridge are the only two universities in Europe which still retain the mediaeval collegiate system. Under the Tudors the colleges narrowly escaped dissolution, to survive as societies of celibate clerical Fellows from the Middle Ages until near the end of the nineteenth century, when Fellows were first allowed to marry.

More religious Orders arrived during the last decade of the century. The Austin Friars occupied a site to the east of St. Bene't's church, the Friars of St. Mary settled at Castle End, and in 1290 the Gilbertine Canons of Sempringham were given a large property, including the chapel of St. Edmund, near the present site of Addenbrooke's Hospital. Tension between the University authorities and the Friars arose at Paris, Oxford and Cambridge, the only universities to have a full faculty of theology. At Cambridge, there were differences in 1303 when the University gave to the Masters legislative powers previously held by the faculties, and the influence of the Friars in the faculty of theology was greatly diminished. The mendicant theological schools did not accept the authority of the Regent Masters, and the problem persisted until the dissolution of the religious houses in the sixteenth century.

In 1318 a Papal Bull of John XXII decreed that Cambridge should be a *Studium Generale*, with Masters and scholars having the rights of a *Universitas*. Henceforth, its Masters were licensed to teach in any Christian land. The University was to be independent of the jurisdiction of the Bishop, and although the Chancellor's right to exercise the powers of absolution and excommunication was later questioned, it was eventually confirmed. The University continued to gain power at the expense of the town. In 1305 the Chancellor obtained the right to summon townsmen to answer scholars in personal actions, and he could imprison in the castle any layman convicted of bodily violence.

The University charter of 1317 required the Mayor and bailiffs, on taking office, to swear to maintain the privileges of the University.

The townsfolk bitterly resented this requirement, and during a riot of 1322 they assaulted scholars, attacked their hostels, and slew a priest. In 1337 the burgesses protested against the powers given to the University, saying that townsmen who injured scholars were punished, but that scholars who harmed townsmen were acquitted. The University, for their part, accused the town authorities of neglecting their duties; they complained that the streets were not kept free from filth and dirt, that the King's Ditch was a danger to public health, and in 1331 they petitioned Parliament to force the Mayor and bailiffs to cleanse it.

The Black Death reached England in 1348, and the disease was at its height in Cambridge between April and June of 1349. At King's Hall, 16 of the 40 scholars died, and the parishes of St. Giles and All Saints by the Castle were united because most of the inhabitants of the latter had died of the pestilence. During the twelfth and thirteenth centuries, a number of large houses, some built of stone and with extensive grounds, were put up between the High Street and the river, and it was here that the next colleges were established.

Michaelhouse was founded in 1323 by Hervey de Stanton, Chancellor of the Exchequer to Edward II, for a Master and seven scholars. He purchased a large house at the junction of Milne Street and Le Foule Lane, and the advowson of St. Michael's church. He rebuilt the church to serve for both collegiate and parochial needs, with a large choir for his student-priests. More land and the sites of two hostels were acquired, the transactions being completed by 1353, and about 20 years later 12 rooms and a kitchen were built. In time, a library was added, and the college probably then formed a three-sided court.

From at least 1317, Edward II maintained 12 children from the Chapel Royal at the University, to provide educated men to serve in the administration. Edward III increased this benefaction in 1336 and purchased a large house belonging to Robert de Croyland on land extending from the High Street to the riverside hythes, to accommodate 32 scholars. King's Hall was a larger foundation than Peterhouse, Michaelhouse or University Hall, the next college to be founded. King's Hall and Merton College at Oxford were the largest English colleges until New College, Oxford, was established in 1379. This

first royal foundation probably influenced other founders and benefactors to turn to Cambridge, although the University at Oxford was
then larger and more renowned. During the 35 years after 1317,
seven colleges were established in Cambridge, but only two at
Oxford.

King's Hall and its scholars had a privileged position in the University, and the college and its Fellows were exempt from the authority
of the Bishop of Ely and the Archbishop of Canterbury. The food was
better than in the other colleges, and tablecloths were provided. It was
the first English college to have a large quota of undergraduates, and
in making provision for learners rather than for teachers, it was a
notable exception to the general rule. The statutes prohibited the
frequenting of taverns, the introduction of dogs, the wearing of short
swords and peaked shoes, and the use of bows, flutes and catapults.
Lectures were being given in King's Hall during the early fifteenth
century, and several of the Fellows were each responsible for the
finances of a number of pupils; this was to become a feature of collegiate life in the post-Reformation period. Additions to the buildings
were slowly made, but almost the only part still existing is what is
now the Great Gate of Trinity, begun in 1519 and completed in
1535.

In 1326 the University obtained a royal licence to settle scholars in
two houses in Milne Street, on part of some land given by Nigel de
Thornton. To the south stood the church of St. John Zachery, and to
the north a hostel acquired by the Prior of Ely to accommodate monks
attending the University. The new college was called University Hall,
but by 1336 the revenues were only sufficient to support 10 scholars.
Two years later it was refounded by Lady Elizabeth de Clare, a grand-
daughter of Edward I. On the death of her brother, the Earl of
Gloucester, at the battle of Bannockburn, she and her sisters had
inherited a great estate. She proposed that the college should have
undergraduates as well as a Master, 20 Fellows and graduates.

Early college buildings were constructed with clunch quarried from
nearby chalk hills. There is no good building stone around Cambridge,
but a great deal of clunch, which is easy to carve and suitable for
internal work. Where it was used externally, it had to be later refaced
with brick or a more durable stone.

THE LATER MIDDLE AGES 1346–1400

Pembroke Hall, Gonville Hall, Trinity Hall and Corpus Christi founded.
Student life and quarrels with the town

Four Colleges were planned between 1346 and 1349. Pembroke Hall was founded in 1347 by the Countess of Pembroke, who was descended from Henry III. On the death of her husband after only a few years of marriage, and very rich, she devoted herself to religion and good works. In 1342 she bought land in Trumpington Street outside the King's Ditch, and acquired more in 1351, when the University gave a hostel to the south. The site was only large enough for a small court, 90 feet by 45 feet, but it contained chambers, a chapel, hall, kitchen and the Master's rooms. The claim has often been made that Pembroke was the first college to have a private chapel, but papal permission was also given to Trinity Hall in the same year, 1366, to hold services in the 'chapel built'.

Edmund Gonville, a priest and the son of a Frenchman domiciled in England, founded Gonville Hall in 1347. He purchased three pieces of land in what is now Free School Lane and obtained permission to establish a Hall for a Master and 20 Fellows. When he died in 1351, he left money to his principal executor, William Bateman, Bishop of Norwich, for the enlargement and endowment of the college. Bishop Bateman changed its name to the Hall of the Annunciation of the Blessed Virgin Mary, drew up statutes, and removed the college to a new site at the corner of Milne Street and St. Michael's Lane, exchanged with the Guild of Corpus Christi. In Milne Street the site extended southwards to what is now Senate House Passage, and in St. Michael's Lane, more than halfway to the High Street. The main entrance was in the Lane, then an excessively filthy thoroughfare. Existing houses provided accommodation for the Master and Fellows for some time. The Bishop had spent many years at the Papal court of Avignon, and he wished the college to provide more clergy trained in canon and civil law to fill gaps caused by the Black Death.

The College of the Scholars of the Holy Trinity of Norwich, or Trinity Hall, was founded in 1350 by Bishop Bateman. Here again he wished to train more lawyers for the Church and the State. He intended to have a Master and 20 Fellows, 10–13 civilians and 7–10 canonists, but when he died in 1355 only a Master, three Fellows and two scholars were in residence. The site of the new college was beside Clare Hall, between Milne Street and the river. At first the college made use of existing houses, but building was in progress in 1352, and the east side of the court and the Hall were finished by 1374.

The College of Corpus Christi and the Blessed Virgin Mary is unique because it was founded by two of the town guilds. The guilds of Corpus Christi and the Blessed Virgin decided to amalgamate, and, in the words of Fuller, 'Thus being happily married, they were not long issueless, but a small college was erected by their united interest'. The new foundation was intended to train persons fitted to make 'supplications to God for the souls of every one of the Fraternity as he departed out of this life'. A royal licence was obtained in 1352, and a site near St. Bene't's churchyard secured. In the following year, the advowson of the church and a house in Luthborne Lane (now Free School Lane) were acquired, and more land further along the lane when the exchange was made with Gonville Hall. The original endowments supported only a Master and two Fellows, but more benefactions in the fourteenth century allowed the number to be increased.

The construction of the Old Court, the first closed quadrangle in Cambridge, began before 1352, and was probably completed by 1378. The entrance was through a simple archway in the north range. This single small court, which has not been greatly altered, was the main building of the college until the nineteenth century. Until the end of the fifteenth century, when two small chapels linked the college and the church, St. Bene't's was used for worship. Until New Court was built in 1827, Corpus was usually known as Bene't College.

The University buildings known as the Old Schools developed from lecture-rooms in a number of houses. The site was given in 1278, but the Divinity School, the first building specifically erected for teaching purposes, was not begun until about 1350. It was built of rubble, and was not completed until about 50 years later. Other modest constructions arose around a court between 1430 and 1474.

Some students wore their hair long, curled and powdered, and had long beards. Those who could afford it dressed more like soldiers than priests, with brightly coloured cloaks, costly girdles hung with knives, and rings. In 1342 Archbishop Stratford issued an order that no student should receive any ecclesiastical degree or honour unless he should reform his person and apparel. The present B.A. or M.A. gown and hood is derived from the ordinary clerical dress of the thirteenth century, although then it was not exclusively clerical and was usually green, blue or red. The long blue coat and yellow stockings, red leather girdle and white bands worn in modern times by the boys of Christ's Hospital gives an idea of the picturesque dress of mediaeval students.

In spite of their colourful clothes, the fourteenth-century students were not comfortably lodged. Early college buildings were very primitive. At Corpus, interior walls were not plastered, the windows mostly unglazed, the ground floors were of clay, and the first-floor rooms had no ceilings. No college rooms were heated, and only the Masters and Doctors had a chamber to themselves. Fellows and Bachelors shared a room with one, two or three students, not only because accommodation was scarce, but to serve educational and disciplinary aims. There were only a few benches in the schools, and the boys usually sat on the straw-covered floor. Roads were bad, and many students came from places a week's journey from Cambridge, so most of them rarely returned to their homes. They often journeyed in the care of a 'fetcher' who collected groups from distant parts of the country.

In 1380, when the population numbered about 3,000, there was again considerable tension in the town, and violence broke out during the Peasant's Revolt in June of the following year. The townsmen had grievances not only against landlords and government officials, but also against the University and the colleges. A hundred years earlier, no colleges had existed, and the University owned practically no ground in the town, but now there were eight colleges owning much property. On Saturday, June 15, rioters destroyed the house of a country landowner and seized his goods, horses, sheep and pigs. At 10 o'clock that night they destroyed the house of William Wigmore, one of the Esquire Bedells, then the mob raided Corpus, burnt its books and charters, and sacked houses belonging to burgesses, University and college property.

Corpus college had been founded by townsmen, but had become unpopular because it had allied itself with the University. Many houses had been bequeathed to Corpus and it owned more property than any other college, A particular grievance was the exaction of 'candle rents', i.e. a tax on town houses originally levied to supply lights for the services of the guilds, but which had now been diverted to the ordinary purposes of the college. One half of the houses in the town were subject to this tax. The attack on the college may also have been partly prompted by resentment against the display of wealth during the great annual Corpus Christi procession of the Host through the streets.

On Sunday morning, a mob went to Great St. Mary's during mass, seized jewels and vessels, broke open the University chest, and burnt the muniments contained in it. At the Carmelites' house they broke open another chest and seized books and property. The Mayor and bailiffs then compelled the Masters and scholars of the University to sign deeds, sealed by the seals of the University and of all the colleges, whereby they renounced all the privileges granted to them by the kings of England, and promised to conform to the law and custom of the Borough of Cambridge, to pay the costs of any litigation between the University and the town, and to abandon all actions against the burgesses. University charters and deeds were burnt in the market place. On Monday a crowd of 1,000 men armed with axes and swords broke down walls and did other damage at Barnwell Priory, the result of grievances about the enclosure of common lands. The rioting was ended when the Bishop of Norwich entered the town with a body of armed men.

A number of commissions investigated wrongs done by the rebels to the University, the Prior of Barnwell and others. Two of the ringleaders were hanged, and others punished. On the complaint of the University, the Mayor and bailiffs were summoned to appear before Parliament at Westminster, and the deeds forcibly obtained from the University were cancelled. The King took back into his own hands the franchises of the town, but restored them a year later, although the jurisdiction over the purchase and sale of food and drink, hitherto held by the town, was given to the University. Sturbridge Fair was expressly included. The farm of the town was increased from 101 to 105 marks. The disorders of 1381 embittered relations between the University and the town; both had suffered injuries that were remembered for centuries, and the joint supervision of trade led to disputes that continued until 1856.

In 1385, more than 100 houses were destroyed by fire, but in the following year the Guildhall or Tolbooth was rebuilt. A hall, an aldermen's parlour, a kitchen and a pantry were supported on arches, and the space below was used to weigh goods brought to the market, in order to levy tolls. This building continued to be used for 400 years. The Chapel of Gonville Hall, built of clunch faced with brick, and smaller than the existing Chapel, was finished in 1393. The Small Bridges in Silver Street are first mentioned in 1396, when the Bishop of Ely granted an indulgence to persons who contributed to the repair of them and attended service in the bridge chapel. There were then two distinct branches of the river. In 1399, Henry IV sent greetings to John Laye, the hermit, and gave him permission to levy customs for the upkeep of the bridges and the causeway. Carts shod with iron wheels were forbidden to cross. Throughout most of the next century, Cambridge was not very prosperous, and in 1402 the burgesses told the King that they were unable to pay the customary farm of the town.

THE LATER MIDDLE AGES 1400–1500

King's, Queens', Catharine Hall and Jesus founded

IN 1400, when the Divinity School was completed, the University acquired the first building to belong entirely to it. Rebuilding began at King's Hall late in the fourteenth century, and by 1400 the college possessed a stone Hall and a timber Kitchen. A Library was added later. King Edward's Tower, begun in 1428 and finished in 1432, was the first example of a monumental entrance, a feature copied later at King's, Queens', Christ's and St. John's, though not adopted at Oxford. King's Hall later built a second fine gateway, now the principal entrance to Trinity. By the end of the fourteenth century, the typical Cambridge college plan of a court consisting of a gateway, a hall and buttery, a kitchen, chapel and sets of chambers, had been evolved, and the colleges built during the fifteenth century adhered to these arrangements.

6 Queens' College: an Exterior Wall of First Court (1448

7 (overleaf) King's College Chapel from the South (1446-15

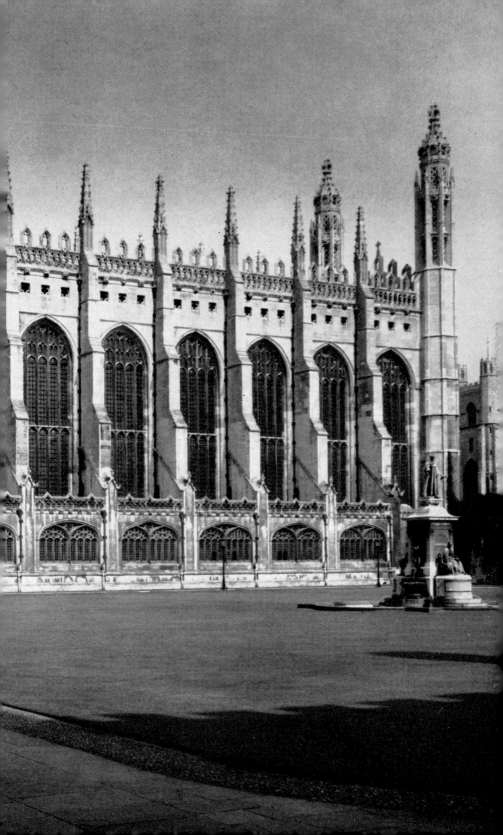

For the first 200 years of its history, the University had been far less important than that at Oxford, but during the fifteenth century Wycliffite heresy there caused royal and other patronage to be transferred to the more orthodox University at Cambridge. By the end of the century, Cambridge probably had as many scholars as the older University. Although great advances were made, it was not an outstanding period. As a result of civil and foreign wars and other difficulties, the number of students increased slowly. After Corpus Christi was founded in 1352, there were no other new colleges until Godshouse, founded in 1439 by William Bateman, a London parish priest, for training grammar school masters. In 1428 the Benedictines obtained two houses in the parish of St. Giles for the accommodation of monks resident in the University, and in later years, various houses of the Order built Buckingham College.

The first royal foundation came into being when Henry VI, then only 19, signed letters patent in 1441 for a new college for a Rector and 12 scholars. This first modest plan was enlarged in 1443 when the King, who had founded Eton College three years earlier, stated that it was his intention that scholars of Eton, when sufficiently instructed in grammar, should proceed to King's. A garden, only 40 by 25 yards, belonging to Trinity Hall, behind the partly completed Old Schools, was obtained in 1440 to form the nucleus of the site, and although in 1443 this was enlarged, it was still very cramped. The King was now contemplating a much larger college with more magnificent buildings, and made plans for 70 scholars under a Provost. The new college was granted extraordinary privileges, including exemption from the jurisdiction of the Archbishop of Canterbury, the Bishop and Archdeacon of Ely, and the Chancellor of the University.

The site upon which the King intended to build was intersected by Milne Street, from which other thoroughfares ran to the High Street and to the river. It was thickly covered with houses, hostels, the parish church of St. John Zachery, and on the centre of the Chapel site, the college of Godshouse. The King proceeded to buy up all this property, and Godshouse was removed to St. Andrew's Street. In 1445 the Mayor and Corporation granted all the streets, the common land beside the river, and the quay called Salt Hythe to the King, and other private property seems to have been easily acquired. Only a draper, who owned

Jesus College, the Gatetower (c. 1500)

two houses on part of the site chosen for the Chapel, held out for a high price, and did not sell his property until 1452.

The large site in the heart of the town was thus obtained by a drastic clearance of thoroughfares and buildings, and the town was cut off from much of the river trade upon which depended a great deal of its prosperity. The King granted the town land to make a new access to the river, the passage now called Garret Hostel Lane. The demolition of many dwellings, and the numerous houses inhabited by students, caused many craftsmen to leave Cambridge; the burgesses claimed that the town was unduly burdened, and in 1446 the Mayor and Corporation secured a remission of taxation on account of the loss of revenue. For the recreation of the scholars, the town granted to the College the common meadowland on the west side of the river, extending from Garret Hostel Lane to the present ditches of King's and Clare.

The first college buildings behind the Old Schools were begun in 1441, but this court was never finished according to the original design, because the King had decided to erect larger buildings on the new site. The Gateway was intended to be of great splendour, but it was not carried beyond the second storey, and only the south range and part of the west range were completed. Owing to the restricted site, the buildings had three storeys. The College expected to move before long, but in fact the old buildings continued to be used until 1828. The original plans were for a small court like the other mediaeval colleges, hemmed in by streets and houses. The King's new plan envisaged magnificent buildings to dominate the High Street, and surrounded by spacious grounds. Henry VI's vision introduced an entirely new concept.

The first buildings included a small Chapel which collapsed in 1536 or 1537. The King did not come himself to lay the foundation stone 'for the aier and the Pestilence that hath long regned in our said Universite', but sent the Marquess of Suffolk. A Provost's Lodge, east of the present Chapel, was built by 1450, and with alterations and additions it existed until 1828. The Founder's statutes of 1443 placed 'at least two Fellows or scholars in each of the upper chambers, three in each of the lower chambers; each occupant is to have a separate bed; one of the Fellows is to be older than the others and is to exercise authority over his chamber-fellows and to report on their manners, conversation and progress in their studies'.

The King's new plan envisaged a magnificent court on the site of the present Front Court, the Chapel to form its north side. The east range, with rooms in three storeys, was planned to have a Gate-tower in the centre. Other ranges would contain living-rooms, a Hall, Library, and Lecture-rooms. A smaller court west of the Hall would have a kitchen, brewhouse, bakehouse and stables. Between the Chapel and the river, the plan provided for a cloistered cemetery and a lofty bell-tower.

The King laid the first stone of the new Chapel in July 1446, but about 80 years elapsed before it was finished. A white magnesian limestone from south Yorkshire, conveyed almost the whole way by water, was used for the earliest part, and by 1461 the stonework had risen to about 60 feet at the east end, and sloped away westward to no more than seven or eight. Little more was done for 15 years, until donations enabled work to be resumed. From 1480 to 1485, work proceeded well, and by 1483 five eastern bays were complete up to the battlements and covered with a timber roof.

In 1446 Andrew Dockett, Rector of St. Botolph's, obtained a royal charter to found the College of St. Bernard for a President and four Fellows, on a site now occupied by St. Catharine's, but soon a larger site on the other side of Milne Street was secured. In 1448 the founder persuaded Queen Margaret, then only 15 years old, to ask leave of her husband to refound and rename the college, because 'in the whiche Vniursite is no college founded by eny Quene of England hidertoward'. The foundation stone of the Queen's College of St. Margaret and St. Bernard was laid in 1448, and the First Court, the earliest existing Cambridge quadrangle of real architectural beauty, was much more ambitious than those erected hitherto. The plan adopted closely resembled that of Haddon Hall. In the fourteenth century, the nobility began to build quadrangular country houses, and colleges adopted a similar disposition of the essential buildings arranged around a court.

When Edward IV became King, Dockett secured the patronage of the new Queen Elizabeth, who granted the first statutes in 1475. The modern spelling Queens' commemorates the two royal ladies who aided the college. Additional buildings, with a cloister on the inner side, were erected beside the river in about 1460. No other college possessed more than a single court until after the Reformation.

Catharine Hall, the name by which it was known until 1860, was founded in 1473 by Robert Woodlark, Provost of King's. The site was the north-west corner of the present court, facing Milne Street, in which the main gate remained until the eighteenth century. The original buildings, all subsequently demolished, formed a small quadrangular court. In his statutes, Woodlark said, "I have founded and established a college or hall to the praise, glory and honour of our Lord Jesus Christ, of the most glorious Virgin Mary, His mother, and of the Holy Virgin Katerine, for the defence and furtherance of the Holy Church, and growth of science and faculties of philosophy and sacred theology'. The college was intended for post-graduate secular clergy. After a time it admitted a few scholars who performed menial duties, and as late as 1743 there was a student porter.

With the exception of the upper part of the tower, Great St. Mary's was completely rebuilt between 1478 and 1519, and only the walls of the chancel were preserved. The University paid most of the cost, partly from current funds, but mostly from special donations. Subscriptions came from Richard III, Henry VII and the Lady Margaret. The church was still roofless when Henry VII and the Lady Margaret visited Cambridge in 1505, and the King gave 100 oaks from Chesterford Park to cover the nave. The tower, begun in 1491, was not finished until nearly 80 years later.

The nunnery of St. Radegund had become impoverished, and when John Alcock, Bishop of Ely, made a visitation in 1487, he found that the conduct of the 11 nuns rendered them unfit to elect a successor to the Prioress who had recently died. He introduced a nun from another house, but when he came again nine years later, he found ruinous buildings and only two women, one a stranger and the other a disreputable character. In 1496 he obtained a licence from Henry VII to suppress the nunnery and establish the College of the Blessed Virgin Mary, St. John the Evangelist, and the glorious Virgin St. Radegund, more usually known as Jesus College.

This conversion of the nunnery is the earliest example in Cambridge of a suppressed religious house forming the basis for a college, and until the early nineteenth century, all of the subsequent colleges

9 *St. Mary's-the-Great, the University Church (rebuilt 1478-15*

appropriated the sites, buildings and revenues of foundations previously existing. Cranmer was a Fellow of Jesus in about 1515, but had
to renounce his Fellowship when he married the niece of the landlady
of the Dolphin Inn and lived with her there. About a year later, when
she died in childbirth, Cranmer regained his Fellowship. If his wife
had lived, he would not have become Archbishop of Canterbury.

THE SIXTEENTH CENTURY 1500–1550

*John Fisher, The Lady Margaret, and the foundation of
Clare and St. John's. The Cambridge Reformers.
Magdalene and Trinity founded*

During the sixteenth century University affairs were dominated by
religious controversies. Hitherto, teaching had been by means of
lectures given by Regent Masters, but as a result of the growth of
colleges, most of it passed into the hands of college Tutors.

The colleges were still small, some on cramped sites. At the end of
the fifteenth century, the buildings and grounds of the religious houses
were larger than those of the colleges. Throughout the sixteenth century, town and gown disputes continued, although an award made in
1503 by arbitrators acting for the Lady Margaret defined the persons
exempt from the jurisdiction of the town magistrates, and the right of
the Mayor and bailiffs to levy market tolls. The University claimed that
excessive tolls were imposed on food and livestock brought into the
town, and that the tolls on carts loaded with building materials for the
colleges were a heavy burden. Thirty years later, the town authorities
complained that because the colleges had become more prosperous and
now had their own bakehouses and brewhouses, the University was
neglecting to control food prices.

By far the most influential man of the time was John Fisher, who
became Master of Michaelhouse in 1497, Vice-Chancellor in 1501, and
was later elected Chancellor for life. In about 1500 he became chaplain
and confessor to the Lady Margaret Beaufort and influenced her to
make important benefactions to the University. She founded the first
professorship, the Lady Margaret Professorship of Divinity, and decided

St. John's College Gatetower (c. 1511)

to enlarge Godshouse. When Henry VI had taken the original site in Milne Street, this college was removed to just outside the Barnwell Gate, and it remained small until, in 1505, the Lady Margaret provided additional buildings and endowments to support 60 members. She changed the name to Christ's College, and constructed the Master's Lodge, Hall, and other buildings to complete the First Court.

She reserved the first floor and attics of the Lodge for herself, or in her absence for Bishop Fisher, and sometimes resided there. Handsome heraldry was placed over the entrance gateway and beneath her oriel window, and the fireplaces had heraldic badges. From her chambers, both the Chapel and the Hall could be observed through small windows. Fuller relates how 'Once the Lady Margaret came to Christ's College to behold it when partly built, and looking out of a window, saw the dean call a faulty scholar to correction; to whom she said 'lente, lente', gently, gently, as accounting it better to mitigate his punishment than procure his pardon; mercy and justice making the best medley to offenders'.

King's College Chapel was finished in the early years of the sixteenth century. Henry VII came to Cambridge in 1506 and gave a large sum to complete the great work of his uncle. The shell was probably finished by 1512, and in the following three years the magnificent fan-vault was constructed. By 1515 the fabric was complete, but the Chapel still lacked fittings. By about 1531 the huge windows had been glazed, and between 1531 and 1535 the wonderful screen and choir stalls, the finest carving of the Early Renaissance style in the country, or indeed anywhere north of the Alps, were put up. Then the floor was paved. Just before the Reformation the Chapel stood complete. Other colleges clung to the Gothic style, in which Trinity built their large Chapel in 1555–64.

John Fisher also persuaded the Lady Margaret to convert St. John's Hospital into a college, but she died before she had made provision for this in her will, and Fisher had to overcome many difficulties to carry out the scheme. The remaining inhabitants of the Hospital were sent to Ely in 1511, and 800,000 bricks were ordered from R. Reculver of Greenwich. The building proceeded rapidly and the college opened in 1516, although the First Court was not completed until 1520. Most of the east front towards the street survives as built, and the west range with the Kitchen, Buttery and Hall is not much changed, although the Hall has been lengthened. The thirteenth-century chapel of the Hospital was refurbished, and a Combination Room and Master's Lodge placed between it and the Hall range.

In the early days of the college the staff consisted of a manciple, two cooks, the Master's servant, a porter, barber, and a laundress who was not allowed to enter beyond the gate. St. John's was a community leading a religious life, and the Chapel services were as important as the academic teaching. Students were only allowed to go out of the college for lectures, and Fellows and pupils, as in earlier centuries, shared rooms. Fisher said that 'the older should advise their younger chamber-mates, give them encouragement and show them good example, instruct them in discipline. . . .' Fisher made St. John's the most important centre of Renaissance learning in the University.

He was the friend and patron of Erasmus, and it was probably he who persuaded Erasmus to live and work in Cambridge for several years. Erasmus, who was the first teacher of Greek in the University and the first textual critic of the Bible, took up residence at Queens'. The new learning of the Renaissance began to reach England in the second half of the fifteenth century, and at Cambridge the humanist movement steadily gained ground after his departure. Lectureships in philosophy, logic and rhetoric were founded in 1518. In 1520, after a visit by Cardinal Wolsey, the University publicly burnt the books of Martin Luther.

John Siberch, the first Cambridge printer and a friend of Erasmus, was probably in the town from 1520 to 1523. University stationers had existed for some time, and in 1534 royal letters patent enabled the authorities to appoint three stationers and printers or booksellers to manufacture and sell approved books. In the early part of the century most of these men were foreigners. One of the booksellers appointed in 1534 was Sygar Nicholson, who had been imprisoned five years earlier when the works of Luther and other prohibited books were found in his house.

The Cambridge reformers met to discuss the new doctrines at the White Horse Inn near the site of the Bull in King's Parade. The most prominent were Robert Barnes, prior of the Austin Friars, and Hugh Latimer, a Fellow of Clare. In 1525, during a sermon in St. Edward's

Church, Barnes attacked the pomp of bishops and the church courts. He was accused of heresy, arrested and taken to London to be examined by Cardinal Wolsey, and tried at Westminster. He eventually submitted and performed public penance at St. Paul's, but was not allowed to return to Cambridge. Latimer and others were also brought before Wolsey. The University, asked to pronounce on the legality of Henry VIII's 'divorce', found for the King, though only if the previous marriage had not been consummated. The Vice-Chancellor admitted that 'All the world almost cryeth out of Cambridge for this act and specially on me', and many others were critical.

The University disclaimed the papal authority in 1534 and Fisher was executed. Thomas Cromwell became Vice-Chancellor, and the Crown began to intervene in University affairs. The colleges were subjected to the royal supremacy and government interference became frequent. There were quarrels with the town, especially regarding the power of the University to excommunicate officials judged to have infringed its privileges, and the necessity for the Mayor and bailiffs to swear to maintain the liberties of the University. In 1529 the Vice-Chancellor excommunicated the Mayor because he refused to answer a charge that he had violated the privileges of the University. He was forced to do penance in the church of the Austin Friars 'holding a candle, the price of a halfpenny in his hand, and kneeling on his knees openly before the image of our Lady'. The excommunication was not rescinded until he had made submission in writing.

After a serious affray between the proctors and townsmen at Castle End, the University renounced the right to excommunicate in temporal causes, but in 1535 and 1537 the town authorities were warned not to press the matters in dispute and the King himself intervened. From 1529, the Reformation and the rise in prices strained the financial resources of the University. The number of students declined, and the disappearance of the monks and friars was a serious blow. Many learned but poor men had to leave the University, and richer young men, many of whom did not take degrees, began to appear. At this time St. John's was the leading college. Five regius professorships in divinity, Greek, civil law, Hebrew and physic were founded in 1540.

In 1538 the University suggested to the King that the monastic buildings should be converted into colleges, but it was not until 50 years

later that the Franciscan and Dominican buildings were used. Barnwell Priory, the oldest and most wealthy of the religious houses, was
surrendered in that year, and the houses of the Friars were dissolved
at about the same time. The University wished to continue to use the
hall of the Franciscans for its commencement ceremonies, but the
King granted their buildings to Trinity. The Dominicans' site was
leased to a townsman. The Carmelites surrendered their house to
Queens' but the King did not recognise this, and divided the site
between King's and Queens'. The house and grounds of the Austin
Friars were sold in 1545 to Dr. Hatcher, Regius Professor of Physic, a
rich man who lived in considerable style in the former Friary. Buckingham College was included in the dissolution, and in 1542 Thomas
Lord Audley was granted a licence to found in its place the College of
St. Mary Magdalene for a Master and eight Fellows.

The Paving Act of 1544 described the town as well inhabited and
replenished with people. This local Act required every householder to
repair, and in some cases to pave, the street opposite his house. Paving
Leets were held twice-yearly in Great St. Mary's, when citizens were
nominated to inspect the streets, and offending householders were
fined. Refuse was allowed to accumulate in the thoroughfares, and the
custom of bringing cattle, pigs and horses into the town at night, and
turning them out on the common pastures in the morning, rendered
'the high stretes and lanes within the same Towne excedyngly noyed
with fylth and myre lying there in great heapes'.

There was an insurrection at the time of Ket's Rebellion in Norfolk
in 1549. Wool had become the principal export, common land was
enclosed for sheepwalks, and the change from arable farming to the
rearing of sheep led to unemployment. The common pasture near
Cambridge was insufficient, aldermen had a prior claim on the use of
the commons, and many leading burgesses had enclosed land. The
poorer inhabitants said that the commons should be let and the rents
applied to their relief. On July 10 a crowd pulled down fences at a
Barnwell enclosure belonging to a former bailiff, and further violence
was only narrowly averted. Some of the rebels were hanged, but as a
result of the protest it was established that the poor inhabitants of the
crowded tenements had a right to use the commons. The town fields,
cultivated in small plots by many owners, reached to the boundaries

of Coton, Madingley, Cherryhinton, Ditton, Barton, Grantchester and Trumpington.

In 1545, an Act for the Dissolution of the Colleges threatened them with the fate of the monasteries, but Henry VIII was persuaded to allow them to keep their possessions after a commission of enquiry had reported that they were so poor that they could scarcely meet their expenses. In December 1546, the King decided to found a college to be called Trinity, for a Master and 60 Fellows and scholars. Michaelhouse, King's Hall and some hostels surrendered their property, and large revenues, chiefly derived from suppressed religious houses, and new privileges were granted to Trinity. Foul Lane, from the end of Milne Street to the gate of King's Hall, was closed in 1551. Some of the old buildings were retained, and a new Chapel was begun in 1555.

Hamond's map shows the state of the college in 1592, a year before Dr. Thomas Nevile became Master and began extensive rebuilding. By 1599 he had completed ranges of chambers on the east and south sides, and then demolished the part of King's Hall which projected into the court. In the north-west he removed some comparatively recent buildings, extended the Master's Lodge to the north, and built a Library towards the Chapel, with two storeys of chambers below it. King Edward III's Gate was taken down and rebuilt between the Library and the Chapel. These alterations resulted in the largest college court in the country. The Fountain was begun in 1602, the new Hall in 1604 and the Kitchen a year later. At his own expense, Nevile built a second court of two parallel wings, with the upper storeys carried on open arches, and the ends of the two ranges joined by a wall with a large gateway.

Statutes of 1549, during the reign of Edward VI, made new provisions for the government of the University and changes in the course of study. Undergraduate diversions such as card-playing, fencing, and wandering about the town were circumscribed. Martin Bucer of Strasburg became Professor of Divinity and for a short time he was an influential figure. When he died in 1551, his funeral was attended by about 3,000 people. On the death of Edward VI two years later, the Council proclaimed Lady Jane Grey as Queen and took steps to arrest the Lady Mary, who stayed at Sawston Hall before she went on to Framlingham. On July 15 the Duke of Northumberland was sent to

Cambridge with an army of 8,000 foot and 2,000 horse, but his men deserted him, and on July 19 Mary was proclaimed Queen in London. The Duke finally proclaimed Mary at the market cross, but he was soon afterwards arrested in King's, taken to London, and executed.

All of the Heads of Houses except three were removed, and candidates for degrees had to subscribe to the Roman Catholic faith. At St. John's, 14 Fellows had to go into exile. Latimer, Ridley and Cranmer, three bishops who had been educated in Cambridge, were burned alive at Oxford, and in Cambridge John Hullier, a former scholar of King's, suffered similarly on Jesus Green. The bookseller Sygar Nicholson gave him gunpowder to end his torture, and 'His flesh being consumed, his bones stood upright, even as if they had been alive. Of the people some took what they could of him, as pieces of bones. One had his heart, the which was distributed as far as it would go; one took the scalp and looked for the tongue, but it was consumed, except the very root.'

By the middle of the sixteenth century poor students were increasingly excluded by the sons of the rich. Latimer wrote in 1549 that 'There be none now but great men's sons in Colleges and their fathers look not to have them preachers'.

THE SIXTEENTH CENTURY 1550–1600

John Caius. The Elizabethan Statutes and the visit of
Queen Elizabeth. Recreations restricted. Hamond's
plan of the town

In a sermon delivered at St. Paul's Cross in 1550, Thomas Lever, a Fellow of St. John's, described the poverty of students. They rose between 4 and 5, went to chapel between 5 and 6, then studied until 10, when dinner was 'a penny piece of beef among four, having a few porridge made of the broth of the same beef with salt and oatmeal and nothing else'. After dinner they again studied until 5, when supper was not much better than dinner. There was more study until 9 or 10, 'and these being without fires, are fain to walk or run up and down half an hour, to get a heat on their feet before they go to bed'. He spoke of

'200 students of divinity, many well learned . . . which be now gone home: and many young toward scholars, and old fatherly doctors'. Many students helped with the harvest or did road-making during the vacations.

There were, nevertheless, many well-to-do young men who intended to become men of affairs. In the Middle Ages, the primary function of the University had been the training of clerics, but now government had become more complex and there was a need for men educated in the new humanist learning. The mainly military character of the mediaeval conception of a gentleman's education was no longer adequate. In 1559, William Cecil, no doubt recalling his own student days at St. John's, suggested that the nobility should be compelled to educate their sons. College Tutors had a close personal relationship with their students, as each supervised only about half a dozen. Bad communications often made it difficult for Tutors to keep their boys supplied with money. Cambridge was still a small town; in 1587 there were only 4,990 inhabitants, excluding members of the University. These probably numbered about 2,000, and new buildings had to be put up to provide sufficient accommodation.

Something entirely new in college architecture appeared soon after Dr. Caius decided in 1557 to refound and enlarge his old college, 'that pore house now called Gonville Hall', where he had become a Fellow at the age of 23. He studied medicine at Padua under Versalius and became a professor there, then visited other Italian cities before he returned to England to practise medicine in London and to become physician to Edward VI and Mary. For his college, where he was Master for 14 years from 1559, he began to design noble additional buildings in which he combined practical considerations with a love of symbolism. In Italy and France he had studied Renaissance architecture, which he wished to introduce into Cambridge. He constructed a new Second Court with buildings on only three sides, the fourth having a wall with an ornate gateway, 'lest the air, from being confined within a narrow space, should become foul'. Henry VIII's palace of Nonesuch had a similar plan.

The walls were of clunch, faced with stone brought from Ramsey, with attractive stone chimneys set diagonally. Henceforth, towers were sometimes built over passage-ways beween courts, and the Gate

of Virtue, erected in 1567 in a pure Renaissance style, is important in English architecture. The Gate of Honour was executed after the death of Caius, but to his designs, and was completed in 1575. One of the statutes of Dr. Caius imposed a fine on anyone who should throw dirt or offal into the court, and his will stipulated that 'there be mayntayned a lustie and healthie, honest, true, and unmarried man of fortie years of age and upwards to kepe cleane and swete the pavementes'. It is related that Caius, 'being very old, and living only at that time on woman's milk, he, while he lived upon the milk of an angry, fretful woman, was so himself; and that being advised to take of it of a good-natured patient woman, he did become so beyond the common temper of his age'.

A new Visitation in 1557, when Cardinal Pole was Chancellor, examined the Heads and Fellows of colleges, investigated whether church ceremonies were being conducted in a proper manner, and burnt heretical books. Because Martin Bucer had been buried in Great St. Mary's and Paul Fagius in St. Michael's, divine service in these churches was forbidden. The bodies of the German reformers were exhumed, and their remains were burnt in the market place. On the following morning, Great St. Mary's was reconciled by the Bishop of Chester and another of the Visitors, and on the next day after there was a great procession through the streets. New statutes were made, but these were superseded two years later when another Commission appointed by Queen Elizabeth restored the Edwardian statutes. The Vice-Chancellor and the Heads of Houses were given supreme control, and the University continued to be governed by these statutes until the middle of the nineteenth century. The new reign brought drastic changes, and many Heads were dismissed. The Elizabethan statutes forbade dice and, except at Christmas, cards; daily resorting to the town; vain clubbing of money; sword-playing, fencing and dancing-schools; gaming-houses; cock-fighting, bear or bull-baiting; quoits; or looking on at any of these.

A new royal charter of 1561 increased the privileges of the University. The Chancellor's court was given power to adjudicate in almost all cases involving members of the University and 'privileged persons'. By 1589 these included anyone who served the University— stationers, bookbinders, illuminators, parchment-makers; apothecaries,

Caius College, the Gate of Honour (1573-5)

physicians and surgeons; bakers, brewers, butchers, gardeners; the children and servants of graduates; and even 'he who times the University clock' and 'one plumber who shall serve the use of the University'. All of these persons were exempted from royal taxes except an annual payment of £10 for the assize of bread.

The University controlled markets and fairs, and could appoint 12 preachers, and these privileges were confirmed by an Act of 1571. Sturbridge Fair was originally granted to the Leper Hospital of St. Mary Magdalene, which by 1279 no longer had any patients. A century later, the burgesses took the considerable profits derived from lettting booths, and although the King seized the franchises in 1538-9, the Corporation was able, some years later, to purchase the grant of the Fair. From 1553 until 1587 the town made continual attempts to obtain complete control, a matter of great importance, since Sturbridge had grown to become by far the largest and most famous fair in all England. In the fourteenth century ships came from the Hanseatic ports, and galleys from Venice and Spain. Charters of 1589 defined the rights of the town and the University; the town was given control of the fair, all the profits from tolls and rents of booths, and dispensed justice, but the University retained many privileges.

Queen Elizabeth visited Cambridge for five days in 1564. In preparation for her coming, roads were covered with rushes, churchyards with sand; the Corporation mace was regilded, the market cross repaired and painted, and the gallows mended. The Queen came on horseback from Haslingfield, 'dressed in a gown of black velvet pinked' and 'a hat that was spangled with gold, and a bush of feathers'. She was met near Newnham by the Mayor and aldermen, but when the procession reached King's the town officials had to leave as they had 'no authority or jurisdiction in that place'. All the doctors and scholars were drawn up between Queens' and the west door of the Chapel. In the Chapel decorated with tapestries and rich crimson velvets, the Public Orator delivered a long speech. When the Queen visited other colleges, she listened and sometimes replied to a great many speeches in Greek or Latin, there were disputations and plays, and a contemporary said that 'If the Queen were weary at the Comedies (as no doubt she was, they being meanly performed), she dissembled her uneasiness very artfully'. She enjoyed her visit so much that she would have been willing to stay longer, but the entertainment of her retinue and their numerous servants had exhausted all the beer and ale in the town. The University of Oxford sent its Proctors and chief Bedell 'to see and hear, as near as they could, for their better instructions (if it should fortune the Queen's Majestie to visit that Universitie) all our doings, order and proceedings'.

Dr. Caius wrote that there were 18 hostels when he first resided in Cambridge between 1529 and 1539, but 20 years later some had been merged in colleges and 'most part are deserted and given back to the townsmen'. The number of Pensioners, i.e. undergraduates who paid for their accommodation, greatly increased, and in the last quarter of the sixteenth century colleges began to build or to improvise pensionaries to house them. In 1569 Corpus adapted the old tennis court for chambers; in 1584 St. John's converted a storehouse, and five years later, houses opposite the main gate. Pensionaries were provided at Caius in 1594 and at Christ's in 1613. Two of the most interesting college buildings in Cambridge, the President's Gallery at Queens' and the Library of Trinity Hall, were put up in about 1570 and 1580.

Regent Walk, or University Street, leading from the west door of Great St. Mary's to the main door of the Schools, was constructed at the expense of Archbishop Parker in 1574. Hitherto, the only direct approach had been by the narrow East Schools Street. In 1575, arrangements were made to light the streets in the evenings between November 1 and February 2 'in such place and places and at such charge as the Vice-Chancellor and the Mayor shall appoint, except such nights as the moon shall shine'. The fish market was moved to Peas Hill in 1579 and it remained there until 1949. On the Market Hill, meat was sold on the south side near the Guildhall, corn, poultry and butter on the north side, and fruit and vegetables in the centre.

After the Dissolution, the house of the Dominican Friars belonged to several different people until it was purchased in 1583 to form the site of Emmanuel College, founded by Sir Walter Mildmay, Chancellor of the Exchequer to Queen Elizabeth. There were extensive grounds and some good buildings. The former monastery chapel was converted into the Hall, and another building, after considerable repairs, became the Chapel. A long range with short wings was built on the St. Andrew's Street frontage, and another building was constructed on the south side of the present Front Court. Ralph Symons of Westminster, who was to put up many other buildings in Cambridge, was employed on this work, and by 1589 the college was almost complete. The founder intended the college to provide educated clergy, and early in the seventeenth century it became the principal home of Cambridge Puritanism.

Many of the restrictions imposed upon the recreations of the students also limited those of the townsfolk. In 1575 the Privy Council ordered the Vice-Chancellor to prohibit 'showes of unlawfull, hurtfull, pernicious and unhonest games' within five miles of the town. Games at Howes on the Huntingdon Road were stopped in 1581 although they had been licensed by the county magistrates. There was a riotous ending to a football match between students and men of Chesterton, when the villagers picked quarrels with their opponents and attacked them with staves which they had hidden in the church porch. It was later alleged that the head constable encouraged the Chesterton men 'to beat the scholers down', and for this crime he was imprisoned in the castle. The Vice-Chancellor and the Heads of Colleges forbade students to play football except in their own colleges.

In 1595 the Vice-Chancellor forbade students to 'walke upon the Market Hill or sitt upon the Stalls', or to go in the streets unless sent on necessary business by a Tutor. 'No student was to wear long or curled locks, great ruffes, velvet Pantables, velvet Breeches, coloured nether Stockes, or any other coloured apparell', and 'that the hurtfull and unscolerlike exercise of Football and meetings tending to that end, do from henceforth utterly cease'.

To accommodate the increasing population, houses were divided into small tenements, and in 1584 the Privy Council instructed the Mayor and the Vice-Chancellor to prevent landlords from doing this. In 1596 the townsmen alleged that 220 graduates were engaged in trade, yet paid no Borough duties or charges. Every inn had to be licensed by the Vice-Chancellor, and in 1597 he reduced the number of alehouses from 80 to 30. John Hamond's plan of 1592, measuring 47 in. x 34 in. gives an interesting pictorial view of a town still small, but with a few open spaces in the centre, and enables us to form an accurate assessment of the density of the buildings. The plan is so detailed that even dovehouses, sundials and pumps are shown.

The Market Place was an L-shaped area and remained so until after the great fire of 1849. There were shops and houses in the churchyard of Great St. Mary's, their outbuildings extending to the east wall of the church, and a narrow alley divided them from a block on part of the present Square. Hamond depicts the old inns, most of them with a narrow street frontage, and a large gateway leading to a long courtyard. Back gates in another street provided an exit for waggons which could not turn in the narrow yards. Some inn yards eventually became public thoroughfares; thus Market Passage was once the yard of the Black Bear, and Rose Crescent that of the Rose and Crown.

To the west of the river, Hamond's map shows the Town Green extending from Queens' to St. John's, except for a paddock belonging to King's. The college grounds along the east bank were enclosed by walls, leaving only a narrow halling-way for horses pulling barges. In one respect Hamond anticipated the future; he shows corner turrets and pinnacles on the tower of Great St. Mary's, although these were not put up until a few years later.

The first University Printer was Thomas Thomas, a Fellow of King's, who from 1583–8 occupied a house and shop in Regent Walk. He was followed by John Legate, who also rented two shops adjoining the west end of Great St. Mary's, and later by Cantrell Legge, with a house on Market Hill. Leonard Greene, appointed in 1622, had a shop 'at the south side of the steple' of Great St. Mary's, and in 1625 was in partnership with Thomas and John Buck. Thomas Buck leased the Angel Inn in Market Street, and after Greene's death in 1630, he hired and later purchased part of the former Augustinian Friary. In partnership with Roger Daniel, he printed Milton's *Lycidas* and, in 1629, the first Cambridge edition of the Authorised Version. He was succeeded by a second John Legate and then by John Field, a protégé of Cromwell. In 1655 Field built a printing house on land now occupied by the Master's Lodge and garden of St. Catharine's.

Another former monastic house became the site of a college when, in 1594, the executors of Frances Sidney, Countess of Sussex, obtained the ground that had belonged to the Franciscans and founded a college for a Master, 10 Fellows and 20 scholars. Most of the buildings of the Friars had been destroyed, but the refectory was divided into two floors to serve as the Chapel, with a Library above. Ralph Symons erected two ranges of buildings on the north and south sides of an open court, and on the east side were the Hall and Master's Lodge. These buildings still exist, although they were altered early in the nineteenth century. The original statutes clearly stated that young men were to be trained to instruct the people in the Christian faith.

The Second Court of St. John's was built in 1598–1602, and it is not much changed today. At Trinity, the Hall and the Fountain were put up in 1600–2, and Nevile's Court in 1606–14. Orlando Gibbons, then 12 years old, became a choirboy at King's in 1596. The great composer subsequently became organist of the Chapel Royal and of Westminster Abbey.

THE SEVENTEENTH CENTURY 1600–1640

The Little New River. Plagues and Plays. The
Town Lectures. The Butt Close controversy

In the small congested town there were frequent outbreaks of plague, and the University had to send students away in 15 years of the sixteenth century. An epidemic of 1573 led Archbishop Parker to suggest that water should be conveyed from Trumpington Ford to the King's Ditch in order to scour it. He said that if this were done, 'no City would be finer than Cambridge, and the memory of so great an Action would not be so grateful to Posterity as pleasing to the Inhabitants'. At about the same time Dr. Perne, Master of Peterhouse, made similar suggestions and submitted plans to the Chancellor.

Nothing was done for 30 years, but in 1606 a number of people, including Hobson the carrier, planned to bring water from the Nine Wells near Shelford into the town. An artificial channel called the Little New River was made from Vicar's Brook near Long Road to the conduit head at the corner of Lensfield Road, and branches supplied water to the fountain in the Market Place, ponds in Christ's and Emmanuel grounds, and to Pembroke. The flow of water was insufficient to scour the King's Ditch, but the 'new river' provided drinking water, and the Market Place fountain supplied people living nearby for 250 years. The fountain, eventually removed to the corner of Lensfield

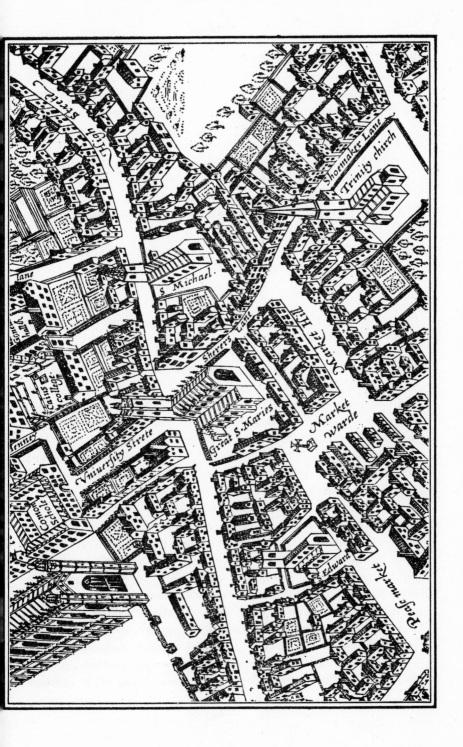

Road, is known as Hobson's Conduit, although he was only one of a number of persons who planned and carried out the project.

The phrase 'Hobson's choice' originated because he kept 40 horses for hire, and always insisted that the animal that had rested for the longest time should be taken out. From 1570 to 1630, when he died at the age of 86, Hobson's large 6- and 8-horse waggons conveyed goods and mail between Cambridge and London, and the journeys over bad roads took three days or more.

Between 1630 and 1645 there were nine epidemics. Refuse was allowed to accumulate in the narrow streets, and in spite of the 'new river', most of the drinking-water was obtained from shallow and polluted wells. The Fens reached almost to the town, and between 1607 and 1653 both the University and the town opposed draining schemes because it was feared that they would cause the river to dry up. Nevertheless, the Earl of Bedford and promoters known as The Adventurers began drainage operations in 1631. At Sturbridge Fair, thousands of people camped without sanitary arrangements, and in the town, 'seges or privies' were placed over the King's Ditch and other streams. In 1616 the University complained that the Corporation had begun 'to build and pester every lane and corner of the town with unwholesome and base cottages', and several Privy Council orders during the next few years forbade the town authorities to cram more houses into every open space, or to divide buildings into small tenements. By 1632 these subdivisions provided accommodation for 1,728 additional persons in six parishes. The colleges, too, were overcrowded; at Sidney in 1623, 130 men were living in 35 rooms.

There was a serious outbreak of plague in 1630, the University was closed, and the Vice-Chancellor wrote; 'Myself am alone, a destitute and forsaken man, not a Scholler with me in College, not a Scholler seen by me without'. 40 booths for infected persons were erected on Midsummer Common, and 5,000 poor people almost starved because villagers would not bring in provisions, nor would they allow townsmen to go to fetch them. To alleviate distress, the town and the University jointly established a 'house of correction' in 1596 to give employment to the poor. In 1628 Thomas Hobson founded a charitable trust to build a Spinning House on the present site of the Police Station, to provide work for the unemployed and to serve as a house of correction for rogues and vagabonds. It was also used as the Vice-Chancellor's prison for prostitutes, and it existed until 1901. A visitor in January 1776 found 6 girls who had been imprisoned with no fire and sleeping on straw, for six months.

The colleges and members of the University were exempted from local taxes, and the introduction of poor rates gave the townsmen another cause for complaint, although the University made a voluntary contribution. In 1632 the Borough obtained powers to levy rates on residents, but scholars and privileged persons were exempted. When the land tax was introduced in 1700 it did not apply to the sites of colleges, but the University agreed to pay a ninth of the total sum required from the town. In 1604 the University gained the right to send members to Parliament who could help to maintain its privileges against attacks from the town.

A charter of 1605 strengthened Queen Elizabeth's charter of 1561; students and privileged persons gained exemption from jury service, and University officials were given power to prohibit bear-baiting, bull-fighting and the performance of plays in English within five miles of the town. In spite of the restrictions on the entertainments of the townsmen, play-acting within the colleges on special occasions was the most common form of amusement. In 1594 the Vice-Chancellor asked Lord Burleigh to lend the royal robes kept in the Tower of London, as there were 'in the Tragedie sundry personages of greatest estate to be represented in auntient princelie attire'. The plays were often coarse, and sometimes satirised the town authorities. Several plays were performed when James I stayed at Trinity in 1614–15, and 2,000 spectators somehow managed to get into the Hall. As some of the performances lasted for seven hours, it is not surprising that during one of them the King fell asleep. Queen Elizabeth must have had greater stamina, as it was said that she always 'watched out'.

There was always great competition to secure tickets for the annual plays performed in the Hall of Trinity during the 12 days of Christmas or soon afterwards, and in 1610 a serious riot occurred at Trinity Great Gate. There was bad feeling between the men of Trinity and St. John's, and when some of the latter attempted to enter the rival college, they were attacked by 'Stagekeepers' armed with clubs and swords. 'Whereupon', said the parish constable at the subsequent enquiry, 'some schollers did cry out for Clubbs, and not long after there were many long clubbs, and pieces of iron and cob-rakes brought into the street'. The arrival of the Vice-Chancellor produced a temporary lull, but when he had departed, stones were thrown from the top of the Gate. A wall was demolished and its materials used as ammunition. The battle went in favour of the St. John's men, and 'the stagekeepers were beaten into the college gates with long clubbs . . . and durst noe more come out of the gates, but divers continued flynging of stones out of the garden, or from the topp of the tower'. At the enquiry held later, a number of scholars were ordered to be suspended or whipped, and five townsmen were 'to be committed to prison, and then brought out to the stage made at the bull-ring, and thereupon to be set in the stocks'.

Apart from the plays, there were few other diversions. Tennis, bowls and archery were popular with only a minority, and there were not many other opportunities for outdoor exercise. The University authorities issued decrees forbidding the new vice of tobacco, the wearing of gaudy clothes, and wandering abroad without leave of a Tutor.

From about 1610 to 1640 there were more students than during the next 200 years, and colleges were enlarged to house them. Queens' put up Walnut Tree Court in 1616–18, and the Sidney Clarke Building in 1628. St. John's built the Library range between the Second Court and the river, employing a mason from Northamptonshire named Grumbold. He and other members of the family worked on many later Cambridge buildings. For St. John's Library, Perpendicular and Elizabethan styles were abandoned in favour of one which is a very early example of the Gothic Revival. A representative of the college said that 'men of judgement like the best the old fashion of church windows, holding it most meet for such a building'.

At Emmanuel, John Westly put up the pleasing Brick Building with Dutch gables at each end in 1634, and from 1635 Peterhouse began to face with stone and decorate in a lively Baroque style the simple Chapel erected in 1628; loggias on either side linked it with other buildings. The Gostlin Building at St. Catharine's dates from 1634–36, and the Fellows' Building at Jesus from 1638–40. Early in the seventeenth century the land known as 'The Backs' came completely under college ownership. St. John's acquired land beyond the river in 1610, laid out a bowling-green and a tree-lined 'long walk'. Trinity obtained a field in exchange for £50, a farm, Parker's Piece and other land in 1612–13, but the college had begun to enclose and plant common land before this transaction.

James I was again lavishly entertained in 1624, and during this visit the marriage treaty between the Prince of Wales and Henrietta Maria of France was signed. The University was predominantly royalist, but the Puritans had great influence, although their position was so insecure that some went abroad. University men formed a high proportion of the early emigrants to New England, and of about 100 who went from Cambridge, 35 were Emmanuel men, and one of them, John Harvard, gave his name to the college in the new Cambridge.

Only a small number of the clergy were licensed to preach; the majority were only allowed to read the prescribed service. A type of service known as a Lecture, and consisting mainly of a sermon, was popular, and Cambridge organised a town lecture at Holy Trinity Church. The lecturers, appointed by the Mayor, were men of academic distinction. Citizens from all parishes subscribed towards the erection of an additional gallery in 1610. The popularity of the 'Town Sermons', which were held at the same time as the University sermon at Great St. Mary's, alarmed the Bishop of Ely and the University authorities. These lectures continued until about 1750.

All of the students were expected to attend both morning and afternoon Sunday services at the University Church, but were forbidden to go to other churches. In 1636 the attention of Archbishop Laud was drawn to the unseemly nature of the Disputations held in Great St. Mary's. He was informed that the Prevaricators made profane and scurrilous jests, and Dr. Barrow, Master of Trinity 1672–7, is believed to have protested that the church was deformed with scaffolds erected for spectators, and defiled with rude crowds and outcries.

A bitter quarrel between King's and Clare arose in 1637–8 concerning Butt Close, now the avenue and garden of Clare. The land belonged to King's, and was used by the scholars for exercise, and for the grazing of horses. The buildings of Clare were in such a poor state that it was decided to rebuild, and the college proposed to set back the new front range to give more light and air both to themselves and to King's, and a better view of the Chapel. In recompense, Clare wished to have a passage through Butt Close to gain access to the fields. King's would probably have acquiesced, but Clare petitioned the King and also asked for a large piece of ground. After a long and acrimonious controversy, Clare obtained the tenure of Butt Close, and built their bridge, the first classical bridge in Cambridge, in 1639–40. The east range of the new court was completed by 1641, and the south range built in 1640–2. Work on part of the west range was halted owing to the Civil War. Christ's began an important new range in 1640, the Fellows' Building, a large symmetrical block standing quite apart. It is of three storeys, with dormers above, and was the first in Cambridge to have the upright type of window.

THE SEVENTEENTH CENTURY 1640–1700

The Civil War and the Restoration. Fellow-Commoners and Tutors

In 1640 Cambridge chose Oliver Cromwell to be one of its representatives in Parliament. Charles I visited the town in 1642 and subsequently asked the University to send him money and their college plate. The Parliamentary party took steps to intercept the plate at a point on the road to Huntingdon, but the University authorities learned of this plan, and a part of the treasure was safely conveyed to the King at York by a Fellow of Clare. Cromwell reached Cambridge in time to prevent the despatch of the remainder. He organised the defences of the town, improved the fortifications of the castle by demolishing 15 houses and remodelling the earthworks. Brick barracks were built for a garrison of about 300 men, and 10 'brave pieces of ordnance' were mounted. Garret Hostel Bridge and five college bridges were destroyed, and only the Great Bridge was spared.

Cambridge became the headquarters of the Eastern Counties Association formed to defend East Anglia, committee meetings were held at the Bear Inn, and the orders of the Association were printed in the town. Cambridge was of great military importance during the Civil

War, since it commanded the roads between the Parliamentary stronghold in East Anglia and the Midlands. In February 1643, when the royal army was believed to be advancing towards the town, Cromwell raised a force of 30,000 men. After the threat passed, a garrison of 1,000 remained. Discipline was lax, and the troops did a great deal of damage to University buildings in which they were quartered. At St. John's 200 prisoners were lodged in the First Court. Soldiers occupied the colleges, and King's Chapel was used as a drill hall. The war and the dismissal of many Fellows disrupted the life of the University, and in 1644, 29 Fellows were ejected at St. John's and only 9 new students were admitted.

A petition of the University to Parliament stated that 'Our Schools daily grow desolate, mourning the Absence of their Professors and their wonted Auditories. . . . frightened by the Neighbour Noise of War, our Students either quit their Gowns, or abandon their Studies'. In 1643 the colleges were forced to contribute to Parliamentary funds, and in the following January, the Earl of Manchester was sent to Cambridge to enforce the Covenant and regulate the affairs of the University. Only men who had taken the Covenant were allowed to hold a college office, and Heads of Houses and Fellows with Royalist sympathies were imprisoned or dismissed. In December 1643 and January 1644, William Dowsing destroyed many 'monuments of superstition and idolatry' in college chapels and parish churches. After the Battle of Naseby in June 1645, Royalist forces occupied Godmanchester, 15 miles from Cambridge, and advanced within two miles of the town, but when the Parliamentary troops marched out to meet them, the King withdrew to Oxford.

The triumph of Puritanism drove the clergy from the churches, and in 1649 only St. Andrew-the-Less still retained a minister, although there were preachers at Little and Great St. Mary's. When George Fox came in 1655 he was assaulted by scholars and had to be rescued by the Mayor. It is believed that the Quakers have been established on their present site at the junction of Jesus Lane and Park Street since 1659. The Friends were persecuted during the Commonwealth, and in 1660 there were 67 Quakers in the local gaols.

The first stage coach to run between London and Cambridge set out from the Devil Inn in 1653, and two years later a coach plied three times a week between the Rose Inn in Cambridge and the Swan in Gray's Inn Road. Hobson's carts carried goods to the Bull in Bishopsgate.

Charles II was proclaimed in the market place on May 11, 1660, first by the Mayor accompanied by the aldermen on horseback, and 'more audibly' by the Town Clerk. On the following day a second proclamation was made when 'the Vice-Chancellor and all the Doctors in Scarlet Gowns the Regents and the Non Regents and Bachellors in their hoods turned and all the Schollars in Capps went with lowd Musick before them to the Crosse on the Market Hill. . . . The Musick brought them back to the Schooles again and there left them, and went up to the top of King's College Chapell, where they played a great while. . . . all ye soldiers were placed round on top of their Chapell, from whence they gave a volley of shott'.

The University gladly returned to its Royalist outlook, and Heads of Houses and Fellows who had been ejected were able to resume their former positions. The Act of Uniformity of 1662 required Masters, Professors and Fellows to declare that they adhered to the Anglican liturgy and that the Solemn League and Covenant was an illegal oath. The town authorities also felt the impact of the Restoration, and commissioners appointed under the Corporation Act removed the Mayor, seven aldermen and 13 common council men. An event of the same year shows that college encroachments on common land were bitterly opposed. When Trinity leased more land beside Garret Hostel Lane and began to build a wall to enclose it, it had to be guarded at night to save it from demolition by angry townsmen. The college accounts record expenses for 'Three warrants about breaking downe the new wall, and for men watching to prevent mischiefe'.

By the middle of the century, men were being influenced by the new ideas of Galileo, Francis Bacon and Descartes, and a group known as the Cambridge Platonists condemned religious dogmatism, although all of its leading members except Henry More were men educated at Emmanuel in Calvinistic Puritanism. The members of this group had a great influence on English thought, and Canon C. E. Raven has said that the whole scientific movement owes a debt to 'the wise, liberal and reverent teaching of the Cambridge school'.

A striking addition to the buildings beside the main road into the town was made in 1663, when the young Christopher Wren was commissioned by his uncle to design a new chapel for Pembroke. It is his first completed work, and five years later he designed a new chapel and loggias for Emmanuel. Work on the riverside range of Clare began in 1669, and on the Hall range in 1683. At St. John's, a Third Court was built in 1669–73, and the south range is believed to be the first in the University to be two rooms thick. There was still no University building in which important ceremonies could be held, although Oxford had acquired the Sheldonian Theatre. Isaac Barrow, Master of Trinity, unsuccessfully attempted to persuade his fellow Heads to erect a hall, and then, as if to demonstrate what might be done, proceeded to build the magnificent Trinity Library designed by Wren. Barrow, a brilliant mathematician, was also an eloquent preacher, whose sermons often lasted for three or four hours.

St. Catharine's began to rebuild in 1674, and the range facing Milne Street was finished by 1687. Loggan's plan of 1690 depicts a complete quadrangle, although the east range was never built. Loggan's plans are a valuable record of the size and appearance of the colleges at this time. College rooms were poorly furnished, with beds in the centre, and partitions in the corners to provide small studies. Fellow-Commoners, young men of rank, paid higher fees and dined at the High Table. Most of them had no desire to study to qualify for a profession, but came to Cambridge to gain a little culture and make some friends before they took their place in society. They were often admitted when only 12 years old, but may not have actually come into residence until a little later. Nevertheless, there must have been some very youthful students sitting with the dons at High Tables; William Wotton became a Fellow of St. John's when he was only 17. Next in the social scale came the Pensioners who paid for their accommodation, and lower still were Sizars who waited on the other students and performed menial tasks to pay for their education.

For a very long time no women were allowed to enter colleges, although an old and hideous laundress was sometimes employed if no suitable man would undertake the task. The first bedmakers were always elderly, and in the seventeenth century they must have begun work at a very early hour, as Alderman Newton's Diary for 1664 records that a Trinity M.A. 'fell downe the stayres . . . being found dead there lyeing about 5 in the morning by the bedmakers'.

Tutors' posts could be very lucrative. They paid a man's college and University bills and tradesmen's accounts, then rendered an account to his parents. Mr. W. J. Harrison's *Life in Clare Hall, Cambridge, 1658–1713* gives information from the account books of Samuel Blithe, a Fellow for 20 years and Master for 35. Blithe was born poor, but when he died nearly £5,000 in cash was found in his study. One would have to multiply this by at least 15 to obtain the equivalent value today. The cost of dying greatly exceeded the cost of living, as one parent was charged, again multiplying by 15, £89 for his son's expenses during a week's illness, and £224 for his funeral.

Many interesting letters from parents to Tutors have survived. In 1680 one father gave the warning that 'His carriage hath been ill. Let the milliners etc. be forbidden to trust him: he hath clothes enough for a quarter of a year, or two months. Take him off from tobacco, he hath forced it on himself, he neglecteth his study, would run after wenches: I hope you will laugh him out of these things. Task him well for his book; if a strict hand be not kept over him he will do but little. Let him not know of this my writing. . . .''

More attention was given to mathematical studies, and eventually they became the sole means of gaining a high degree. Isaac Barrow, a man of genius, was followed by Newton, who became the first Lucasian Professor of Mathematics in 1663 and lived at Trinity from 1661 to 1696. Two years later, Newton worked out the principles of the theory of gravity, and the first edition of his *Principia Mathematica* was published in 1687. By 1692 anatomy was being taught at Cambridge.

Approximately 30,000 freshmen came to Cambridge during the seventeenth century, but only about 16,000 in the next hundred years. In about 1760 the number of students fell to its lowest figure. Early in the eighteenth century, undergraduates studied classics, divinity and philosophy; the latter included arithmetic, trigonometry, Euclid, astronomy and some physics.

William of Orange landed in England in November 1688, and there were nights of terror in the town when it was rumoured that disbanded Irish troops were approaching to burn houses and cut throats. For several nights lawless mobs did much damage under the pretence that they were searching for Papists.

14 *St. Catherine's College (Late Seventeenth-centu*

THE EIGHTEENTH CENTURY 1700–1760

Richard Bentley. Coffee houses. The river trade.
Hawksmoor's plan. The Senate House. Sturbridge Fair

The first third of the eighteenth century is sometimes called the age of Bentley, because he was by far the most outstanding figure among the college Heads. He was the foremost critical scholar of classical learning of his time, and Macaulay called him 'the greatest man in his own department that has appeared in Europe since the revival of letters'. Richard Bentley entered St. John's as a sizar, then became a schoolmaster and Keeper of the King's Library at St. James'. From 1699–1734 he was Master of Trinity and made many improvement to the buildings. He added a wing at the rear of the Lodge, installed a magnificent oak staircase, panelling, marble fireplaces, and large sash windows. A German scholar, Zacharias Conrad von Uffenbach, whom he entertained in 1710, reported that the Master of Trinity was 'as well lodged as the Queen at St. James', or better'. Bentley contributed £200 towards improvements to the Chapel, and asked the Fellows to relinquish their dividend for a year. He blocked the east window, erected a noble Renaissance altarpiece with large Corinthian columns, and put in splendid woodwork. In those days of compulsory chapel, he himself did not attend for 20 years.

He built a laboratory for Vignani, who came from Verona to be Professor of Chemistry in 1702, and for Roger Cotes, the first Plumian Professor of Astronomy in 1704, he constructed an observatory on top of the Great Gate. It was Bentley, too, who in 1717–18 converted the rough marshlands into what we call the 'Backs'. Although he was the most distinguished Cambridge scholar of his time, he had an extremely overbearing and truculent nature and could not co-operate with others. Throughout his Mastership he quarrelled with the Fellows and the disputes terminated in costly legal proceedings. Bitter personal feuds did great harm to both Trinity and the University.

When the University Press opened a new London office and warehouse in 1937 it was named Bentley House, since it was largely due to his influence that the University set up a press of its own. A syndicate

The Senate House (Gibbs, 1722-30)
The Old University Library (Wright, 1754-8)

of senior members was appointed to govern the new University Press, and a building opposite the gateway of Queens' was partly demolished and the remainder incorporated in a new printing house designed by Robert Grumbold in 1698. The diarist John Evelyn refers to it as 'that noble presse which my worthy and most learned friend [Bentley] . . . is with great charge and industrie now erecting at Cambridge'. John Hayes had succeeded John Field as printer, and it was intended that he should occupy the new building, but he refused to move and the original plan was not carried out until after his death. Grumbold's building became a warehouse, and later served as lecture rooms for the professors of chemistry and anatomy. For some years it was used as an anatomical theatre.

Von Uffenbach was impressed by Trinity Lodge, but he said that the town was as mean as a village, and were it not for the colleges, Cambridge would be one of the sorriest places in the world. He visited the Greek's Coffee House, where he read the journals and met the chief professors and doctors. Oxford claims the first English coffee house, opened in about 1650, but Cambridge must have had one not much later, as Roger North's Life of his brother John, who entered Jesus in 1660, states that there was then one coffee house 'but now the case is much altered; for it is become a custom, after chapel, to repair to one or other of the coffee houses (for there are divers) where hours are spent in talking; and less profitable reading of newspapers'.

North considered this 'a vast loss of time'. Apparently the University authorities took a similar view, as in 1664 it was decreed that men going to coffee houses without their Tutor's leave should be punished. In 1750 a man found in a coffee house between 9 and 12 in the morning could be fined 10s. for each offence. The eighteenth-century coffee houses also sold alcoholic drinks, and customers often lingered for several hours to converse with friends and read the newspapers. In 1711 a student of King's who was the only son of Bishop Fleetwood wished to marry Mary Paris, who kept a coffee house near the college, but the Vice-Chancellor sent her to the House of Correction and informed the Bishop, who was able to prevent the marriage. The Elizabethan building in Trinity Street now occupied by the Turk's Head Grill forms a link with the past, as it was once the Turk's Head Coffee House.

In 1701 the University intervened once again to suppress theatrical shows. Although the Corporation had licensed the performance of plays at Sturbridge Fair, the Vice-Chancellor ordered that the theatre booth should be demolished. 62 M.A.s were enrolled to enforce his decree, and the celebrated actor Doggett, the founder of the Thames watermen's badge, was imprisoned. Somewhat later a county magistrate built a theatre, and by 1748 plays were being performed for three weeks during the Fair.

When Princess Margaret visited the city in 1963, she was entertained to lunch on the river by the Conservators of the River Cam, a body established by Act of Parliament in 1703 to improve the navigation between the Great Bridge and Clayhithe. From the twelfth century until the coming of the railway in 1845, the rivers between Cambridge and the Wash were of very great importance. Corn was being exported to Norway in 1202, and Lynn, which had a big coastal trade with Newcastle and London, was constituted a staple port in 1373 because wool and other products were brought from Cambridge and other places. Disputes over dues were settled in 1535 when the Cambridge merchants were granted an injunction to allow them to moor their ships and load and unload at Lynn. The coal trade began in the sixteenth century. The *Foreigners' Companion* of 1784 stated that Cambridge received from Lynn flesh, fish, wild-fowl, butter, cheese, and all manner of provisions; coal, bricks, timber, tiles, clay, sand, iron, lead, peat, oil, reeds and rushes. Some of the butter was sent on to London by waggon. 'Every Pound of this Butter is roll'd, and drawn out to a Yard in Length, about the Bigness of a Walking-cane; which is mentioned as peculiar to this Place'. Butter was so sold until comparatively modern times.

In 1712 Nicholas Hawksmoor, a pupil and later a collaborator of Sir Christopher Wren, made a grandiose plan for the remodelling of the centre of the town. He was invited to submit designs for new buildings at King's, and it is probably while he was working on these that he conceived a scheme entitled 'The Town of Cambridge as it ought to be reformed'. He planned to pull down one side of Petty Cury and to construct a wide street from the entrance to Christ's to King's Chapel, with a 'Forum' or covered market between Great St. Mary's and St. Edward's Passage. A new University Church would replace St. Edward's, and the Corporation would then have the exclusive use of Great St. Mary's. A Senate House beside the new church would be linked to it by a colonnade. Trinity Street was to be straightened, the Great Gate screened by columns, and a new street made between Trinity and Sidney. A widened St. John's Street would curve round the church of All Saints, and there would be squares on both sides of the road beyond the Great Bridge. Hawksmoor's plan was probably the most visionary scheme ever made for an English provincial town, but it had not been commissioned, no one championed it, and no part of the plan was ever executed.

Although a Senate House was contemplated in 1640, it was not begun until 82 years later. In 1715 George I presented 28,965 printed volumes and 1,790 manuscripts from a collection formed by John Moore, Bishop of Ely. Although the University Library was enlarged, it could not provide enough space for this important gift, so it was decided to alter the Regent House to accommodate books, and build a new Senate House. The University already owned some of the property between Regent Walk and Caius, and in 1719 it appointed a syndicate to make additional purchases between Trumpington Street and the east front of the Schools. Houses on the south side of Regent Walk were slowly acquired from 1723.

A scheme for a three-sided court was proposed by Sir James Burrough, Master of Caius 1754–64, a distinguished amateur architect, and adapted by James Gibbs, the most important architect of the first half of the eighteenth century, who built St. Martin-in-the-Fields 1722–6. From 1722 he designed a number of buildings for the universities, including the Radcliffe Camera at Oxford. The plan for Cambridge envisaged a Senate House on its present position, with an identical building opposite intended to house the registrary and a printing-house, the two wings to be linked by a new library building for the royal collection. Only the Senate House was built (1722–30), and the books were not completely housed until 1752. In the meantime they were not safeguarded, and many were stolen. The destruction of property to make way for the Senate House increased the land tax payable by the parishioners of Great St. Mary's, and after a petition to Parliament the University paid a quota.

While the Senate House was being built, some people violently opposed the projected south building. The Master of Caius said that it was 'a Scheme for which I do in my Conscience believe the whole World will condemn Us; a Scheme that will so effectually shut out all View of that noble fabrick Kings-Chapell, that I wonder how the University or that College can bear it; and a Scheme so injurious to Caius College, that I am fully resolv'd not to bear it'. In the meantime Emmanuel had constructed the large Westmoreland Building, and in 1723 Gibbs began the Fellows' Building at King's. Here again only a single range was built, although the college intended it to form one of three blocks which, with the Chapel to the north, would have made a complete court.

At the beginning of the eighteenth century many of the colleges built of clunch were in bad repair or actually unsafe, and it was necessary either to rebuild or reface them. As a result, some courts lost their mediaeval aspect. The old court of Pembroke was refaced in 1712–17, and between 1728 and 1742 Burrough similarly 'beautified' Trinity Hall. Burrough's best work was the Fellows' Building at Peterhouse, begun in 1736, and just after the mid-century he refaced Gonville Court at Caius and the First Court of Peterhouse.

Most of the students were still ordinands and they were now usually 17 or 18 when they came up. Numbers were still small; from 1734 to 1766 the average number of men taking the B.A. degree was 106. St. John's was the largest college from about 1640 to 1785, then Trinity gained and continued to hold first place. There was much drunkenness among the dons, and many undergraduates gave scant attention to their studies. Men of noble birth could gain degrees without examinations, and most of the Fellow-Commoners led an idle life. Some went riding and shooting, for which the undrained Fens offered splendid facilities. At all times there were, of course, some students who worked assiduously.

Some of the bad roads were improved by private benefactors and by several Turnpike Commissions set up from 1724 to 1745. The Master and Fellows of Trinity Hall were the trustees of money left by a former Master and his executor for the repair of highways, and in particular the road to Barkway. Milestones measured from a disc cut in the South-West buttress of the tower of Great St. Mary's were set up along this road, the first in England since Roman times.

In the middle of the century, a great deal of business was still done at Sturbridge Fair. It then lasted for a fortnight, although it had decreased in importance since Defoe visited it in 1723. He then said that it was the greatest in the world, surpassing those at Leipzig, Frankfurt and Nuremberg, that the goods displayed in booths arranged in rows like streets, came from all parts of England and the Continent. 50 hackney coaches came from London to ply night and morning to carry people to and from Cambridge, and wherries were brought from the metropolis on waggons, to ply upon the river to tow boats to the fairground. Defoe describes the Mayor's procession on the opening day, when he was attended by the two M.P.s and 12 aldermen on horseback, and many others on foot. This ceremony was curtailed in about 1758 and abolished in 1790.

A famous Cambridge character associated with the Fair is Jacob Butler, who in 1714 inherited the Abbey estate at Barnwell, including the field where the Fair was held. He was six feet four inches tall, a graduate who became a barrister and was engaged in numerous lawsuits. In his old age he called himself 'Old Briton' because he fought so strenuously for what he considered to be his rights. Ancient custom decreed that any corn still standing on the fairground on the 24th of August could be trampled down by stall-holders, and booths not cleared away by Michaelmas Day might be demolished. 'Squire' Butler asserted these rights and once drove his carriage among piles of crockery. Towards the end of his life he ordered a huge oak coffin, and when he died in 1765 at the age of 84, his body was taken to the church in a leaden coffin, while the oak coffin followed on a waggon. The wooden coffin was lowered into a vault, and the smaller one then placed inside it.

A Shire Hall was built in front of the Town Hall in 1747; both buildings were raised on pillars so that market stalls might remain below, and they were connected by a wooden bridge. The town defied the University by setting up a bull-ring on Peas Hill, and cock-fighting took place on Market Hill until the end of the century. A newspaper announcement of 1749 declared: 'This is to acquaint the Publick That on Monday next in the afternoon the Great Muscovy Bear will be baited at the Wrestlers' Inn in the Petty Cury'. The University authorities continued to try to keep students away from amusements, and regulations of 1750 provided that 'every person in statu pupillari who shall be found at any coffee-house, tennis-court, cricket-ground, or other place of publick diversion or entertainment, betwixt the hours of nine and twelve in the morning, shall forfeit the sum of 10s. for every offence'.

The original timber bridge at Queens' was constructed in 1749, and Essex rebuilt the town's Great Bridge in stone five years later. James Essex was a local man who worked for the University and many of the colleges, and in 1756 he began the brick riverside building at Queens'. In 1770 he built the new range for Emmanuel that faces St. Andrew's Street. The old Guildhall was demolished in 1782 and replaced by a building designed by Essex. To help to defray the cost, a number of honorary freemen, who each paid 30 guineas, were created. A foundation stone, a Barnack stone over 5 feet long with an inscription, was incorporated in the building, but its position was not known until it was discovered 18 inches below floor level when the present Guildhall was being erected. The stone has now been placed in an interior wall.

The Duke of Newcastle, who became High Steward in 1739 and Chancellor in 1748, exercised a great influence on University affairs for many years, particularly in the appointment of Masters and Professors. University and national politics were closely interwoven. The Duke strongly supported a project to enlarge the Library, and the beautiful east front of the Old Schools was begun in 1755. Burrough prepared the plans, but Stephen Wright was responsible for the elevations and supervised the construction. Proposals for a block to match the Senate House were revived but again abandoned. Two years later, the University bought the property between Regent Walk and East Schools Street still in private ownership, and land to the south was purchased from King's in 1769. In 1762 the University acquired the large garden of the Austin Friars between Free School Lane and Corn Exchange Street for a Botanic Garden. When this purchase was made, its future importance cannot have been realised, since it is on this site that many of the science laboratories and arts lecture rooms were subsequently erected. A lecture room for the Jacksonian Professor and the Professor of Botany was built here in 1786.

The most famous Cambridge printer of the eighteenth century was John Baskerville, who in 1763 produced a folio Bible which has been called 'one of the most beautifully printed books in the world'. His types were purchased by a French society, but in 1953 the punches were secured by the University Press. William Samuel Powell, Master of St. John's from 1765, introduced college examinations. John Jebb, a prominent reformer, strove for several years to persuade the University to hold annual examinations for all undergraduates, including noblemen and Fellow-Commoners, but his proposals were rejected. Most of the dons were under-employed and drunkenness among them was rife.

THE EIGHTEENTH CENTURY 1760–1820

Richard Watson, Richard Porson and Isaac Milner. The
Improvement Commissioners. John Mortlock dictator of
the town. Enclosures. Jesus College founded

By 1760 the average age of entrance to the University was 18, the B.A. Degree course lasted for 10 terms, and examinations were held in January. In the fifteenth century, when 'an ould bachelor' questioned candidates during the Disputations, he sat on a three-legged stool or tripod, and he became known as 'Mr. Tripos'. He conducted his part of the proceedings in verse known as 'tripos verses', and by the middle of the eighteenth century lists of successful candidates were printed on the reverse side of sheets of tripos verses. These lists were called 'the tripos', and eventually the word was used to denote any examination leading to an Honours Degree.

Disputations, mostly on mathematical questions, were still important, and they were said to provide admirable training in the art of presenting, attacking and defending an argument. When Senate House examinations were instituted, the Disputations became less important, but they were not discontinued until 1840. From 1752, the printed results of examinations divided the candidates into Wranglers, Senior and Junior Optimes, or those who had only done sufficiently well to obtain a degree.

College Tutors, one or two in number according to the size of the college, did most of the teaching. A man might become a Fellow at the age of 22–24, and some Fellows held several livings, whereupon they

17 *Trinity Hall: the West Range of Front Court (c. 1352–7*

either neglected their pastoral duties, or became virtually non-resident in college. The incomes of senior men were so low that many resigned their Fellowships to marry or to enter the church or the professions. There was little demand for advanced teaching, and many of the professors did not give any lectures.

References have often been made to Richard Watson, who confessed that he knew nothing about chemistry when he was elected Professor in 1764, or of divinity when he gained that chair in 1771, yet he worked hard to master these subjects. He became a Fellow of the Royal Society, was a successful Tutor, tried to introduce regular examinations, and opposed the award of degrees without examination to Fellow-Commoners. It has also been said that when he became Bishop of Llandaff in 1782, no Welshman ever saw him, but he did in fact perform some pastoral duties, although he lived for most of the year in the Lake District. He appointed a deputy to discharge his University obligations, and remained Regius Professor of Divinity and Bishop of Llandaff until his death in 1816.

He must certainly have been a remarkable man who worked hard in his youth, as he began his academic career as a Sizar, yet became second Wrangler, a Fellow and a Tutor. In his autobiography he says that: 'I had, at the time of being elected a scholar, been resident in college for two years and seven months, without having gone out of it for a single day'.

One of the most remarkable classical scholars of the period was Richard Porson, born in 1759 and the son of a Norfolk weaver. He showed such an amazing aptitude for learning and had such a phenomenal memory that benefactors sent him to Eton and Cambridge. He became a Fellow of Trinity in 1782, but had to relinquish the post 10 years later because for conscientious reasons he would not take Holy Orders. In 1792 he was appointed Professor of Greek, but the stipend was so low that he lived mainly in London. He had a European reputation for his scholarship, but was also a notorious drunkard and became so untidy and dirty that he was often mistaken for a tramp. He died in 1808 and was buried in the ante-chapel at Trinity.

The first occupant of the Jacksonian Professorship of Natural Experimental Philosophy, instituted in 1783 to embrace chemistry, physics, mechanics, metallurgy and applied science, was a most remarkable man. Isaac Milner was apprenticed to a woollen manufacturer, but his

Pembroke College Chapel (Wren, 1663-4)

brother Joseph, seven years older, entered Catharine Hall as a Sizar. When he left Cambridge, Joseph became headmaster of Hull Grammar School, and obtained an usher's post for Isaac, where William Wilberforce was among his pupils. The older brother recognised Isaac's abilities and helped him to obtain admission to Queens' as a Sizar in 1770. When he graduated as Senior Wrangler he was so superior to the other candidates that he was awarded the distinction of 'incomparabiles'. He was elected to a Fellowship, became an M.A. and a college tutor, took priest's orders and became rector of St. Botolph's.

He studied chemistry, contributed papers to the Royal Society, and was elected a Fellow of the Society when he was only 30. As Jacksonian Professor, his lectures, at which he gave many practical demonstrations, were very popular. He paid for a great deal of equipment, and when he became President of Queens' in 1788 he fitted up a room as a workshop and laboratory. Milner was tall and broad, he expressed strong opinions in a sonorous voice, and towards the end of his life he became one of the most colourful and dominating personalities in the University. In 1791 he was appointed Dean of Carlisle and spent about a third of his time there; in 1792 he was Vice-Chancellor.

During most of the eighteenth century there was little improvement in the condition of Cambridge streets. Some people opposed suggestions for better lighting because they thought that it might lead to more fighting between men who now passed one another unrecognised in the darkness. An Act of 1788 set up a body of Paving (later Improvement) Commissioners empowered to cleanse, pave and light the town and to levy rates; it functioned for 100 years. Oil-lamps were fixed to the walls of colleges and houses, and Petty Cury was the first street to be paved with rounded cobbles. In Trumpington Street, two roadside runnels were constructed to replace the dangerous stream in the middle of the road. The Commissioners spent £3,000–£5,000 a year; the Corporation contributed only £10 per annum. The University agreed to pay two-fifths of the sum spent, and by 1854 the growth of the town made their share excessive.

In the meantime, Cambridge gained a hospital destined to become one of the best in the country. John Addenbrooke, a Fellow of St. Catharine's, who died in 1719, bequeathed money to provide a hospital for the poor. Financial and legal difficulties were not surmounted until

1759; four years later the trustees bought a site in Trumpington Street and erected a modest building. To enable the hospital to open in 1766, additional funds were subscribed by the University and by gentlemen of the borough and the county.

Plans to erect a building opposite to the Senate House were again considered in 1783, and a design by Sir John Soane was rejected in 1791. Apparently a majority had now realised that a building in this position would partly obscure the view of King's College Chapel. In the meantime, the buildings on this site had been demolished, enabling Trumpington Street to be considerably widened opposite Great St. Mary's, and Senate House Passage was made. Great quantities of coal, iron, stone and timber were still brought by water from Lynn, but the silting of the river caused the University and the town to combine to ask Parliament to pass a Bill 'for making and erecting Sluices and other Engines on the said river and cleansing and digging the Shallows'. An Act was passed in 1783. Pleasure trips on the river, usually in heavy six-oared boats, became popular late in the century, and there were often fights with the bargemen when students cut tow-ropes.

In a letter dated November 28, 1791, Samuel Taylor Coleridge wrote: 'We have had a dreadful circumstance at Cambridge. Two men of Pembroke quarrelled, went to Newmarket, and the challenger was killed'. There had been no academic duel within living memory, and the tragic result shocked the whole University. At the inquest there was a verdict of wilful murder against Applewhaite, the survivor, and his two seconds. The University expelled him and one of his opponent's seconds who was an undergraduate, but at Bury Assizes the Grand Jury threw out a charge of murder and Applewhaite was acquitted without a trial.

At the close of the eighteenth century, six coaches ran to London and five to other towns, and the waggons of James Burleigh, who has given his name to a street, went to the metropolis five times a week and to other places. During the war with France, Burleigh offered to lend 60 horses and eight waggons to the government. In 1803 when an invasion by Napoleon was feared, another Cambridge carrier offered 100 horses, 12 broad-wheel waggons and 24 flat-bottomed boats with the men and horses usually employed with them, also blacksmiths wheelwrights and collar-makers. The town formed an infantry corps of 450 men and the University a corps of 180; one of the officers was a future Prime Minister, Lord Palmerston. Pictures of the Volunteers in uniform show that they wore top hats.

In the half-century preceding the reforms of 1835 there was a marked deterioration in the conduct of the Corporation, and corruption and inefficiency increased. From 1784 until his death in 1816, John Mortlock was the dictator of the town and was Mayor 13 times. In 1778, when only 23, he purchased the freedom of the borough; he became a councillor in 1780, an alderman in 1782. He founded the first bank in Cambridge and was closely associated with the Duke of Rutland, who represented the University in Parliament from 1774 to 1779.

At the age of 29, Mortlock was returned unopposed to Parliament, and after he resigned his seat in 1788, candidates backed by him and the Rutland family were always elected unopposed until 1818. Mortlock founded the Rutland Club at the Eagle and the Child Inn to counter the aldermen's club at the Rose, and here he entertained magistrates, councillors and freemen who supported the Rutland interest to suppers and dinners. 24 new pro-Mortlock freemen were created in 1784 on the pretext of raising money for the new Guildhall. A further 89 freemen were admitted five years later, most of them Rutland dependants who did not live in the town, but who could be brought in to vote if Mortlock's rule were challenged. He was an honest business man and capable of disinterested actions, but boasted that he played with real men as others moved chessmen on a board. He remarked to a critical friend that: 'Without influence, which you call corruption, men will not be induced to support government'. The Rutland interest remained supreme for 16 years after his death. His eldest son was nine times Mayor, and corruption and the squandering of Corporation property continued unchecked.

The number of students had decreased considerably since the end of the seventeenth century, and there had seemed to be no need for another college; in fact, none had been founded since the end of the sixteenth century. When, however, Sir George Downing died in 1749, he left money for a new college. Litigation caused delays and the college was not founded until 1807. During the long interval, Parker's Piece and Doll's Close (now New Square) were considered as possible sites, but the final choice was Pembroke Leys. The Court of Chancery approved

19 *Emmanuel College Chapel (Wren, 1668-*

plans for buildings more grandiose than could be provided with the available funds, and in consequence the number of Fellows had to be reduced by statutes of 1860 and 1882. The Master's Lodge and East Lodge, with chambers between them, were finished by 1812 to the designs of William Wilkins. Additional buildings were gradually constructed, but the Chapel was not completed until 1953. In the meantime, a large area of the grounds was sold to the University to provide sites for scientific laboratories.

Most of the colleges had their own barber, and Professor Pryme wrote that during his student days (1799–1803) there was a barber's shop just inside the gate of Trinity near Bishop's Hostel, where the Fellows were powdered and had their wigs dressed. 'There were two or three undergraduates who wore powder. The rest of us wore our hair curled. It was thought very rustic and unfashionable not to have it so. Wigs were still worn by the Dons and Heads, with two or three exceptions'.

In 1801 the population of the town, excluding the University, was 9,276, and about 800 undergraduates were in residence. Scarcely any new houses had been added in the previous half-century and the built-up area was only about one mile long and half a mile wide. A comparison of the plans of Cambridge made by Loggan in 1688 and William Custance in 1798 shows that the number of buildings had increased only slightly during the intervening 90 years. In 1798, open fields extended from Barnwell village to the wall of Christ's, and from St. Thomas' Leys to Downing Street. Along Trumpington Road the houses ended at Spittle End (Lensfield Road), and in Regent Street there were no buildings beyond the vicinity of Parker's Piece. When an Act of 1801 extinguished commoners' rights in Pembroke Leys to obtain the site for Downing, this was the first important part of the arable and pasture land encircling the town to be enclosed. Acts of 1802 and 1807 sanctioned the enclosure of Cambridge Field and Barnwell Field, and between 1801 and 1841 the population of the parish of St. Andrew-the-Less increased from 252 to 9,486.

In 1804 the University Press converted a warehouse erected on the south side of Silver Street on the site of the White Lion Inn in 1786 into a printing house. Further extensions followed, and the Press remained in Silver Street until it moved to spacious new premises in

Peterhouse, the North Range of Old Court (1424-5)
⊣ the Chapel (1628-32)
Downing College, the North Range (Sir Herbert Baker
⊣ A. T. Scott, 1930-53)

1963. By 1808 there were 11 schools supported by voluntary contributions. Only two of them taught reading, writing and arithmetic; the others taught only reading. During the peace celebrations of 1814 there was a feast on Parker's Piece at which 5,338 lb. of beef and 700 6-lb. plum puddings were consumed, but it was a period of much unemployment and distress. At a joint meeting of the University and town authorities held in 1819 to establish a Society for the Suppression of Mendicity, it was said that Cambridge had long been infested, especially at the Backs of the Colleges, with beggars and vagrants who extorted money by threats and stole from college rooms and dwelling-houses.

The Theatre Royal at Barnwell was built in 1816, but was allowed to open during vacations only. A new Garret Hostel Bridge built in 1818 by contractors for the Improvement Commissioners had to be rebuilt three years later. Gas was introduced in about 1820, when John Grafton, one of the pioneers of the industry, took up residence in Maids' Causeway. Street lighting by 'oil gas' began in 1823, and a little later Grafton contracted to light the streets with 'inflammable air or gas obtained from coal'.

G. B. Airy has written that when he was a student at Trinity in 1819, dinner was at 3.15, and some of the senior Fellows spoke of the time when it was at 2. Cold suppers were provided at 9 o'clock. The fasts of the Church were supposed to be strictly kept, with no dinner in hall, but this was overcome by holding the evening service at 3 instead of at 5.30; a normal full meal was served at 4, but as it followed the chapel service it was held to be supper.

THE NINETEENTH CENTURY 1820–1845

The size of the town. College Masters supreme.
Boat clubs. The corrupt Corporation

Travellers of 1820 who arrived by coach or post-chaise from London came upon the first houses at the corner of Lensfield Road. Addenbrooke's Hospital was only a small building 'near the south-west end of the town, and most pleasantly situated in the fields and surrounded by physic gardens'. Visitors next passed a row of small houses and shops on the site of the Fitzwilliam Museum, and Peterhouse, visible only over a high wall. The town really began at the corner of Mill Lane, where some travellers would alight at The Cardinal's Cap Inn. From here to Great St. Mary's, the street became very narrow, with houses on both sides. Tenants of the dwellings on the college side of King's Parade were given notice to quit by October 10, 1823, and it was not until two years later that the new buildings of King's and of Corpus replaced domestic property.

Charles Merivale, who became Dean of Ely, entered St. John's in 1826, and wrote in his autobiography that 'The ordinary street architecture of Cambridge was almost uninterrupted from end to end, and most paltry it was. Except for a few superior house fronts in Trinity Street, the whole line on both sides of the way consisted almost wholly of mean tenements'. A number of small houses at the corner of Trinity Street were not demolished until Caius put up the Waterhouse Building in 1868. A narrow way between high walls led to Trinity Great Gate, and an ivy-covered wall partly obscured St. John's, while across the street the tower of All Saints projected into the roadway. St. John's Lane, bordered by houses and ancient college buildings known as the Labyrinth, ran through the site of the Chapel to the river. The Market Place was still L-shaped, not much wider than surrounding streets, and houses and shops encumbered the eastern side of St. Edward's. Corn Exchange Street was a narrow thoroughfare called Slaughter House Lane, with many buildings of this nature on its western side, and the Botanic Garden occupied most of the site of the New Museums. Mill Road was a quiet country street with only one building, Polecat Farm, and Chesterton a village not yet linked to the town.

In 1817 the University unwisely revived the Black Assembly, ostensibly to suppress vagrancy, and this ceremony embittered relations with the town until it was abolished in 1856. In the same year the Vice-Chancellor, James Wood, suppressed the Union Society because it discussed political subjects. Another Vice-Chancellor allowed it to reopen four years later, provided that political events of the previous 20 years were not debated. Wood was another poor boy who gained high academic honours. The son of a Lancashire weaver, he entered

St. John's as a sizar, where he studied by candlelight while sitting on the staircase with his feet in straw, because he was too poor to afford a fire or his own light. He became Senior Wrangler in 1782, Master of St. John's in 1815, and wrote mathematical books used for 30 or 40 years.

After 1819 there were more students at Cambridge than at Oxford. Many colleges were enlarged between 1820 and 1830, and some men had to lodge in private houses. Lodging-house keepers had to be licensed and conform to certain rules. The Neo-Gothic New Courts of Corpus and Trinity, begun in 1823, reintroduced tower gatehouses. Both courts were designed by Wilkins, the most important collegiate architect of his time, and in 1824–8 he built the Hall range and Screen at King's. Wilkins was the son of an architect and was educated at Cambridge. He visited Italy, Greece and Asia Minor and began as a Greek revivalist before he turned to Gothic. New buildings were put up at Jesus, Christ's, Emmanuel and Peterhouse, brick gave place to stone, and revived Gothic or Tudor-Gothic styles were chosen. Lecture-rooms in the Botanic Garden were enlarged in 1823 to provide a museum and lecture-room for anatomy, and the Observatory was built. 'New Town', between Hills Road and Trumpington Street, was developed between 1820 and 1850.

The Evangelical Movement gained many adherents during the first third of the nineteenth century. Isaac Milner was the most important don among its leaders, but Charles Simeon, a Fellow of King's, was the most influential. As vicar of Holy Trinity, he was at first unpopular with his parishioners and undergraduates, who accused him of preaching methodism and disturbed his services, but later he had large congregations. Although Cambridge educated half of the future Church of England clergy, the University provided no official instruction in theology, and Simeon formed societies for this purpose and invited hundreds of men to discussion parties. In about 1820 a group known as 'The Apostles' began to meet to talk about literary and philosophical subjects. Tennyson and F. D. Maurice were early members, and the Society deeply influenced many of the more thoughtful undergraduates.

The Heads of Houses were still supreme and ultra-conservative, and they imposed strict discipline upon the undergraduates. A man who became Master of a college considered himself to have been elevated to an infinitely higher sphere, and would often behave coldly and autocratically towards colleagues who had been old and intimate friends. When a Master gave a dinner party he invited only other Heads of Houses and their wives. At a dinner given by Dr. G. E. Corrie, the Master of Jesus, one of his guests was a tutor, H. A. Morgan; three Masters present were so disgusted that he should be among their select company that they did not speak to him throughout the evening. Dr. Corrie, who died aged 92, declared that he had lived so long because he wore chamois leather vests.

In about 1830 the Masters were so remote from the rest of the University that the wife of one of them asked a professor's wife, 'What do you talk about in your society? Is it amusing?' A new Master of Downing who had lived for many years in London refused to accept the narrow exclusiveness of his colleagues, and began to give musical parties for a wider circle. After one of them a Master's wife remarked, 'Some people came in the evening—of course we went away'.

When a Fellow of Trinity attacked compulsory Chapel services, the Master, Christopher Wordsworth, forced his resignation. He was more enlightened when he supported the introduction of the Classical Tripos in 1822. Hitherto, a man could only gain honours in mathematics. From 1825 men of noble descent were no longer excused from taking the Senate House Examination.

The Corporation levied a toll of 2d on all loaded carts entering or leaving the town, and the tolls were leased to individuals who employed collectors to stand at the chief entrances. In 1824 some of the inhabitants raised a fund to challenge the Corporation in the courts, and when three of the principal firms refused to pay tolls, the Corporation took legal action. A verdict in favour of the defendants deprived it of half of its income.

The river began to be used for sport in 1825, when St. John's and Trinity formed boat clubs. Dean Merivale says that the former's boat was 'of prodigious strength and weight, standing high in the water . . . like a three-decker', and it carried a 'Tin Panthermanticon' containing two kettles, nine plates, four dishes, a canvas table, a charcoal bag and a phosphorous bottle, etc. The Trinity boat, built in London, proved to be in every respect superior when its crew responded to a challenge from their rivals. Coxes blew a bugle to indicate their position to the other crew. By 1827, one ten-oar, two or three eight-oar, and a six-oar boat belonging to Caius, began regular bumping-races. The first Oxford and Cambridge race was held two years later, when the Oxford crew wore dark blue striped jerseys and the Cambridge men had pink sashes. In 1836 the Cambridge crew were in white, but just before the race, a Christ's man bought some light blue ribbon to fasten to the bows. In 1845 the second May boat of Jesus refused to go down to a race because it was raining.

In 1829 Charles Humfrey made *A Report on the Present State of the River Cam, with some suggestions for the improvement of the navigation of it.* Most of the river was only 3 feet deep, and barges had to be restricted to a draught of 2 feet 8 inches and a load of 20 tons. In times of drought, they often took four days to travel from Clayhithe to the mills. To remedy this, the river was deepened, two locks were eliminated, and the Jesus Green lock rebuilt. Even a hundred years ago the Mill Pool was the scene of great activity. Barges loaded with coal, corn and oil-cake were sometimes so numerous that one could step from one to the other from the mills to beyond Queens' bridge, and there were proposals to construct a dock on Corporation land. Granaries covered a large area between Mill Lane and Little St. Mary's Lane, and waggons waiting to load or unload frequently completely blocked these streets.

The Pitt Building in Trumpington Street began to rise in 1831. A public fund to provide a national monument to William Pitt was launched in 1802, and after statues had been erected in Hanover Square and Westminster Abbey, a handsome sum of money remained. A bishop suggested that it should be used to enlarge the University Press, and the administrators agreed to pay for a building to be erected opposite Pembroke, where Pitt had been a scholar. The foundation stone was laid in 1831. The architect, Edward Blore, was official architect to William IV and Queen Victoria, and he designed and built Abbotsford for Sir Walter Scott. The Press used only the wings of the building, and for a time the central part housed art treasures from the Fitzwilliam bequest. From 1836 to 1934 it was occupied by the University Registrary.

A leading article in *The Times* of November 16, 1833, commenting on the enquiry of the Municipal Corporations Commission into local government in Cambridge, said that: 'Probably no judicial investigation into a public trust ever brought to life more shameless profligacy or more inveterate dishonesty, more bare-faced venality in politics, a more heartless disregard of the claims of the poor in the perversion of funds left for their benefit, or a more degrading subservience to the views of the rich when they appeared in the shape of patrons or distributors of places, a more insatiable cupidity in the corporate officers to enrich themselves with the corporate property, or a more entire neglect of their duties and functions as magistrates, than are presented by the evidence now before us.'

The municipal affairs of a population of over 20,000 were controlled by 158 freemen, of whom 40 were non-resident. In the previous 14 years, the Corporation had spent £1,300 from public funds on dinners, and only £480 for public purposes. One alderman had bought Corporation land worth £150 for one guinea; another had paid £40 for two acres in Hills Road, which a year later he sold for £400. A Common Councilman told the Commissioners that he thought that the Corporation had a right to expend their income on themselves and their friends. He said that 'As it was only Corporation property I would not make the same calculation for a stranger as for a friend. I would make a little difference, and sometimes a great difference, in favour of a friend—because it was only Corporation property'. The quays were in bad repair and the bridges unsafe. There was no market-house, and stalls extended into and congested all the streets near the Market Place. So much filth accumulated at the cattle market on St. Andrew's Hill that it was 'oftentimes almost impassable'.

The Municipal Corporations Act reduced the number of aldermen to 10 and increased the councillors to 30, to be elected by the ratepayers. The first elections swept away the former Corporation, and every alderman who stood for re-election was defeated. A police force was set up in 1836. In 1841 the Town Council suggested that most of the commons should be enclosed and let as market gardens or for building plots, but outraged inhabitants met in the Guildhall and persuaded the authorities to abandon their scheme.

Compulsory chapel caused a stir at Trinity in 1838, when the college authorities decreed that undergraduates must attend at least eight times a week, and imposed penalties on offenders. Some of the students formed a 'Society for the Prevention of Cruelty to Undergraduates', kept a record of the attendance of Fellows at chapel, and published the results in a weekly paper sold in Cambridge and London. After six weeks, the Master and seniors announced that six attendances a week would suffice.

An Act of 1844, which remained in force for 50 years, prohibited any theatre within 14 miles of Cambridge. Two years later, when the American dwarf General Tom Thumb was exhibited in the Guildhall, the promotors charged 2/6 in the mornings, when it was assumed that undergraduates would attend, and 1/– in the evening for townsmen. When many students went to the evening performance, they were hustled by townsmen. On the following night there were town and gown fights, and these developed into a fierce battle on the fourth night. The gownsmen attempted to make a stand in Rose Crescent, but were driven to take refuge behind the Great Gate of Trinity, where they spent an uncomfortable night licking their wounds. Windows were broken in several colleges, and order was not restored until the following day, when the authorities swore in a number of special constables.

J. S. Henslow, Professor of Botany and Charles Darwin's teacher, considered that the Botanic Garden was too small and too near the centre of the town. In 1831 the University purchased 50 acres beside the Trumpington Road, and the first tree was planted in 1846. An old gravel pit was transformed into a lake, glasshouses and one of the first rock gardens in the country were constructed in the sixties, and by the seventies the Garden was well established, with many fine and rare trees.

THE NINETEENTH CENTURY 1845–1860

The railway. Student life. The widening scope of studies.
Cricket. The University Press

When the Great Eastern Railway reached Cambridge in 1845, the station was placed so inconveniently distant from the centre of the town on the insistence of the University authorities. There had been earlier ambitious proposals for a line continuing to York, with a station on Jesus Green, or near what is now Latham Road. The Great Northern was also anxious to get to Cambridge, and proposed to have a station either near the Botanic Garden, off Silver Street, or in Emmanuel Road. The Borough Council supported the latter proposal, but the Master of Christ's said that his college and Emmanuel would be rendered almost uninhabitable owing to the continual howling and whistling of engines. The Great Northern finally reached the town in 1866, when they built a separate platform at the existing station.

An Act of 1844 gave the University the right to supervise the movements of students, and Proctors could require the railway company to refuse to carry a man even if he had paid his fare. In 1851 the Vice-Chancellor protested about Sunday excursions to Cambridge, saying in a letter to the directors that 'he expressed his pain that they had made arrangements for conveying foreigners and others to Cambridge at such fares as might be likely to tempt persons who, having no regard for Sunday themselves, would inflict their presence on the University on that day of rest. . . . The contemplated arrangements were as distasteful to the University authorities as they must be to Almighty God and to all right minded Christians.'

A local newspaper reported in November, 1845, that 'We have seen the last of those elegant conveyances, the London coaches, upon which Cambridge used to look with pride. Last Saturday the Beehive ran its last stage: the contest against all-potent steam was found to be useless, and the reins were given up after a struggle of a few months. We are glad to record that the victor has been at least merciful, for Wilkins, the civil driver of the Beehive, has been provided for by a berth upon the rail'.

Although as late as 1860 barges brought coal from Lynn, the coming of the railway disrupted the business activities of many Cambridge merchants who dealt in commodities hitherto brought by water, and caused a great deal of unemployment and distress. Between 1851 and 1854 there were more than 1,000 empty houses, a high proportion when one remembers that it was a time of large families and that the total population was only about 28,000. The mill pool, where barges unloaded goods into warehouses, and a scene of bustle for centuries, became more and more deserted.

The population had increased rapidly, and many people lived in overcrowded tenements with no sanitation. In 1849 a report on the health of the inhabitants stated that 'The conditions are so wretched as to be a disgrace to civilisation; it is next to impossible for the inhabitants to be healthy, moral, decent or modest'. Behind the houses and shops of the main streets, archways gave access to small courts crammed with buildings. About one-sixth of the population lived in courts, alleys or yards, some less than a yard wide, and many in houses without drainage or a water supply. Drinking water was obtained from pumps, wells, the New River and the Trinity College supply, the latter first brought from the Madingley Road by the Franciscans in 1327. Some householders had to go a quarter of a mile to fetch water, and there were owners of pumps who refused to sell it unless people also brought coals or beer.

A spectacular fire in a large group of old houses near the east end of Great St. Mary's in 1849 made it possible to enlarge the Market Place to its present dimensions. The fire-fighters could only obtain water from Hobson's Conduit and from the river at the end of Garret Hostel Lane. Hitherto, much of the chancel of the church had been hidden by houses on one side of the narrow Pump Lane. The east end of St. Edward's was similarly obstructed, and was not completely cleared until 1874.

Students spent about 12 weeks more a year in Cambridge than at present. Trinity and St. John's were by far the largest colleges, their average intake of students in the eight years before 1850 being 135 and 97 respectively. Caius came next with 30, and only Christ's, Corpus, Emmanuel and Queens' had more than 20. The standard of the ordinary degree course taken by more than half of the men was very low. There was no general University entrance examination, and many of the students came up inadequately prepared. Between 1851 and 1906, 23 per cent failed to obtain a degree, and a large proportion of these were men who had come up only to enjoy themselves.

There were only college lectures, and John Venn, who entered Caius in 1853, said that apart from Trinity and St. John's 'there was probably not a single college which provided what would now be considered the minimum of necessary instruction, even in classics and mathematics'. At Caius a mathematician lectured on theology. Students saw their Tutors for only a few moments at the beginning and end of term, and were left very much to themselves. No individual instruction was given, and most men had to go to private Tutors either throughout their residence, or at least just before the examinations. Tutors and lecturers were obliged to take private pupils because they could not live on their official college income, and good men left the University because more secure and remunerative posts could be found in the professions and in the rising public schools. The University possessed only three or four properly equipped lecture rooms, and the Professor of Chemistry had one room to serve as both laboratory and lecture room, and no apparatus.

Most students led a spartan life in poorly furnished rooms; there were oil lamps in the courts and tallow candles on the staircases. In the 1840s, the Hall of St. John's was heated by a charcoal brazier, and in Trinity there was no heating in the Library or the Chapel, and only one brazier in the Hall. Bedmakers were indignant when a student installed a bath in his room in 1853 and required his 'bedder' to fill it every morning with water from the fountain. All examinations were held in January in an unheated Senate House, and some candidates wore two sets of underclothing or two overcoats.

Caps and gowns were worn a great deal, and all day on Sundays, even by those taking long country walks. A letter of 1850 said that 'The chimney-pot was our only headgear besides college caps—and we carried these silk hats with us always, even to the boats', but straw hats with bands of the college colours, known elsewhere as Cambridge or Varsity Boaters, were popular; a directory of 1850 lists 12 actual makers and 11 shops specialising in the sale of them. Some of the richer undergraduates had well-furnished rooms and spent large sums on dress, wearing cut-away coats with high velvet collars, embroidered waistcoats, peg-top trousers and chimney-pot hats. Black coats and waistcoats were obligatory for Hall, and men who arrived improperly dressed were liable to be asked to go back to their rooms to change. Dandies had their hair curled, and mutton-cutlet type whiskers were fashionable. Beards and moustaches became popular at the time of the Volunteer Movement in 1859.

'Reading-men', i.e. those who took their studies seriously, did not associate with those others, however cultured and well travelled, who did not intend to do much work. Reading-men went to Chapel at 7 a.m., and all had to attend both services on Sundays. Lectures for Freshmen were from 9 to 11, then came private study until lunch, a plain meal of bread and cheese or a cold pie. There were no teetotallers. Between 2 and 4 o'clock men went for a walk, and those who could afford it rode. Only a few played cricket, football, or went on the river, and golf was unknown. On wet afternoons the cloisters of Nevile's Court in Trinity were thronged with undergraduates and dons who paced up and down.

Dinner was at 4 o'clock, in a Hall inadequately illuminated by gas brackets projecting from the walls. Joints of beef or mutton and dishes of vegetables were placed at short intervals on the tables, and men helped themselves. The hungry and the wise ensured that they arrived in time to sit down in front of a joint, since latecomers were liable to find only a few shreds of meat on the bones. Everyone drank beer, and sweets were available at an extra cost. Bedmakers, wearing black bonnets and shawls, acted as waiters. The period between Hall and evening Chapel at 6 was used for reading, chatting with friends, or a wine-party. After Chapel, reading-men studied until 8 or 8.30 and then had tea. Some would continue to work until bedtime, others would seek the society of their friends. There were far fewer opportunities than now for sport or other distractions, so that little stood in the way of a man who wished to study assiduously. Fellows were not called upon to take any part in the government of the University. They did not have to attend meetings of Boards, Syndicates, or Discussions in the Senate House. They were not allowed to marry. Those who wanted to work and those who preferred to be lazy could both pursue their course undisturbed.

The rules of society ordained that the Heads of Colleges and the Professors must entertain, and there were morning calls, evening parties and dinners. For the latter, about a score of people would be invited to a meal lasting for two hours, food coming from the college kitchen. At this time college cooks were independent tradesmen, and some made large fortunes.

The Amateur Dramatic Club, or A.D.C., was founded in 1855, and for five years rented two rooms in the Hoop Hotel in Sidney Street. It became a recognised institution largely because Edward VII took a great interest while he was an undergraduate. In 1870 the University authorities proposed to suppress the club, but Mr. John Willis Clark drafted rules under which it was allowed to continue.

The Prince Consort became Chancellor in 1847, and soon after his election he advocated that the scope of studies should be widened. The University was still governed by the Elizabethan Statutes, but in 1848 some graduates and former members who believed that changes were necessary asked the Prime Minister to appoint a Royal Commission. A report issued in 1852 suggested many reforms. It recommended the opening of 'avenues for acquiring academical honours in many new and distinct branches of knowledge'. Students should take the Previous Examination and then study for one of the triposes or an ordinary degree. The scope of legal, medical and theological studies should be widened, and honours courses in civil engineering and modern languages should be provided. All main subjects should have a board of studies. The Commission found that the smaller colleges could not provide efficient teaching, and private tuition could not be abolished unless the standard of lecturing could be improved. There should be more professors, who must live in Cambridge for at least six months of each year, and only those who gave lectures should receive a salary. More lecture rooms and laboratories were needed, especially for scientific studies; the Commission was told that in the current year, only two or three men took up the study of medicine because facilities in London were greatly superior. The annual income of the colleges was ten times that of the University, and the colleges ought to make a contribution towards general University expenses to help to pay for more professors, lecturers and new buildings.

In 1851 King's ceased to maintain the right of its students to obtain a degree without an examination, but the University was slow to introduce reforms. The Cambridge University Act of 1856 appointed eight commissioners to revise University and college statutes. A Council of the Senate replaced the old Caput, and new boards of studies were established. Members of the Senate had to belong to the Church of England, but men taking degrees in the arts, law, medicine or music were freed from the necessity of a religious test. Laymen could hold college offices and Fellows might marry; professors were required to reside in Cambridge. Members of the University were debarred from voting in municipal elections.

The Town Council had told the Royal Commission that they objected to the necessity for the Mayor to have to swear to uphold the privileges of the University, the right of the Vice-Chancellor to license alehouses, theatres and other entertainments, and the University's right to control weights and measures, to arrest and punish prostitutes, and to discommune tradesmen, i.e. to forbid students to deal with them. The Act of 1856 deprived the University of the right to license alehouses, and to supervise weights and measures, markets and fairs, but it retained the power of the Proctors to arrest prostitutes and of the Vice-Chancellor to license theatres. Both the Vice-Chancellor and the Mayor had to approve occasional entertainments. The Senate House, Library, lecture rooms, laboratories, museums and college chapels and libraries were exempted from parochial rates, but other college property was to be rated. The University contribution under the Improvement Acts was reduced from two-thirds to a quarter. The police were to be controlled by a Watch Committee, with nine town and five University members, the Mayor to be chairman. There was a riot during the parliamentary election of 1856, when a crowd attacked the gates of Trinity and St. John's and entered Christ's, but the Act was a fair settlement of town and gown differences, and made better relations possible.

A period of prosperity for the University followed these reforms, and the average number of freshmen rose from about 400 in 1850 to about double that number in 1880. Between 1861 and 1921 the number of undergraduates increased threefold. Many dons and students had doubts about the orthodox Christian doctrines, and in 1864 Leslie Stephen, Fellow and Tutor of Trinity Hall, left the University and later renounced his orders. Henry Sidgwick, a great scholar, teacher and administrator who has been called the first modern Cambridge don, had grave doubts about religion for many years, and in 1869 resigned from his academic posts. Religious tests, except for Heads of Houses and candidates for divinity degrees, were abolished in 1871; hitherto, a brilliant student who was a dissenter could not become a Fellow.

In the meantime, the Prince Consort sent his eldest son to Cambridge, and the future Edward VII lived at Madingley Hall. In November 1861, when his conduct was causing some anxiety, Prince Albert came to visit him. It was a cold day, and the Prince felt so chilled when he went to bed that he suspected that the sheets had not been properly aired. He died at Windsor a few days later. The Prince of Wales wished to buy Madingley Hall, but as its owner was anxious to remain there, he acquired Sandringham instead.

University cricket was born in the middle of the eighteenth century, when some young men who had learned the game at Eton and Westminster came up to Cambridge or Oxford. The University Cricket Club was not founded until 1824–5, but a University XI played a match against the town in 1820. Fenner began to let his private ground, surrounded by a wall built with bricks from the demolished gaol, to the University club in 1848. When college cricket became popular, only Jesus possessed its own ground, and each college had its recognised pitch on Parker's Piece. In 1860 so many matches were sometimes in progress that the fieldsmen were intermingled, and hits from one game crossed with others. Whewell proposed that Trinity should have a cricket ground in 1862. A number of seedy-looking professionals equipped with a bat, ball and stumps haunted Parker's Piece, anxious to give instruction to students for a small fee. In about 1900 Prince Ranjitsinhji gave handsome gifts to men who helped him to improve his game. He often placed a gold sovereign or half sovereign on top of the stumps, to be won by anyone who could dislodge the coin. Four town players, Hayward, Carpenter, Diver and Tarrant, were in the All-England XI, and in the early 1860s Cambridgeshire was one of the strongest county sides in the country. Sir Jack Hobbs later learned to play the game on Parker's Piece.

Baker's map of Cambridge, published in 1830, marked a solitary brick kiln in the fields on the north-west side of Coldham's Common, but by the end of the century the Newmarket Road ran through a district of brick and tile manufacturers, ironworks, a gasworks, and coal yards. The population of the area of Barnwell, 252 in 1801, increased to 2,211 in 1821, and to nearly 13,000 in 1862. Barnwell had such a bad reputation that the inhabitants asked the Post Office not to stamp the name on letters posted in the district, and no undergraduate not engaged in mission work could be seen there without the taint of suspicion. As late as 1899, when the Bishop of Ely made an appeal for additional clergy, he described it as a 'thickly thronged suburb, a dark spot close upon the very focus of light. Many University servants were living there, and the evil of a large, poor and almost destitute population needed remedying.'

The University Press was considerably expanded during the second half of the nineteenth century. By 1827 the printing house built on the south side of Silver Street in 1804 was too small, and buildings were erected to the west of the courtyard. Steam presses were installed in 1838. The Royal Commission of 1852 reported that 'no Syndicate . . . can replace the vigilant superintendence of those whose fortune in life is dependent upon its success', and the University accordingly entered into partnership with a London printer, C. J. Clay, who controlled the Press for 40 years. After the first ten years he had quadrupled the turnover, and new machine rooms, warehouses and a foundry were built from 1863 to 1878. The grandiose Pitt Building has already been mentioned. In the seventies the Pitt Press series of textbooks was inaugurated to meet the needs of Local Examination candidates.

THE NINETEENTH CENTURY 1860–1900

The Cavendish Laboratory. Colleges for women.
The Statutes of 1882. May Week

Matthew Arnold maintained that in comparison with the German universities, those in England were only high schools. The teaching of science was particularly neglected, and until 1867 no college gave a Fellowship to a scientist. The important Cambridge chemical school began modestly in 1852 when G. D. Liveing fitted up a laboratory at his own expense in Slaughter House Lane. St. John's later built a laboratory for him behind New Court, and he became Professor of Chemistry in 1861. The St. John's lab. existed until 1914, although their physics lab. was closed in 1894. The natural sciences acquired an adequate University building, 1864–5, but there was no accommodation for experimental physics until the seventh Duke of Devonshire provided funds to build the Cavendish Laboratory in 1872–3. For the first six years after James Clark Maxwell became Professor

22 *An elegant Victorian Pillar-box;* 23 *The massive railings*
Senate House Yard; 24 *Ironwork in front of the Fitzwilliam Museum*
25 *Lock gates, Jesus Green*

of Experimental Physics in 1871, the number of students never exceeded 20; by 1885 there were about 100.

Maxwell's successor, Lord Rayleigh, appointed in 1879, found the equipment totally inadequate. There was no steam-engine or other prime mover, and students had to design and make their own apparatus. Rayleigh established a workshop for the manufacture and maintenance of instruments, and engaged a skilled mechanic who had been a Liverpool shipwright. Two of the demonstrators, R. T. Glazebrook and W. N. Shaw, produced *Practical Physics* to overcome the lack of a suitable textbook.

The next Professor, J. J. Thomson, appointed when he was only 28, remained at the Cavendish for 34 years. There was still little money for equipment, and most of the apparatus had to be improvised. Ernest Rutherford, a farmer's son from New Zealand, one of the first graduates from overseas to come to do research, arrived in 1895, and began to work on wireless communication. When he made enquiries about the possible financial prospects of his discoveries, he was told that they were negligible. In 1898 he was appointed to a professorship at McGill University, Montreal. J. J. Thomson discovered the electron, and the Cavendish became the most important research establishment attempting to answer the question 'What is matter?' One of his colleagues was C. T. R. Wilson, known as 'Cloud Wilson' because he was working on condensation experiments with ionised air. When J. J. became Master of Trinity in 1918, Rutherford succeeded him at the Cavendish, and carried out the experiments which opened up the vast new field of nuclear physics. He so inspired his staff and students that, in the words of one of them, he created 'an atmosphere that no one who experienced it will ever forget'.

John Stuart, the first occupant of the chair of Mechanism and Applied Mechanics, established in 1875, erected workshops in Free School Lane. When J. A. Ewing replaced him in 1900 there were practically no facilities apart from workshops crowded with lathes and tools, and Sir Gabriel Stokes lectured in a loft. The old Perse School building became vacant; Professor Ewing persuaded the University to allow him to use it and launched an appeal for funds. Gifts of money and equipment enabled a roof to be erected over the old school yard, and two wings to be added. These developments displeased the Master of Corpus who complained that the noise from a generator disturbed the sleep of his aged horse, and the Rev. D. Skeat, who lectured above the workshop on mediaeval languages, protested about a terrible humming noise coming from the room below.

There was a demand for better educational facilities for women, and in 1868 the Senate instituted a Women's Local Examination. Henry Sidgwick formed a committee to arrange courses of study; he received the support of a number of distinguished professors and lecturers, and in 1873 it became the Association for the Promotion of the Higher Education of Women in Cambridge. Emily Davies began to raise money to establish a college, and 12 of her friends agreed to serve on an executive committee. She insisted that the proposed college should prepare students for the normal University examinations in classics or mathematics. A house at Hitchin was rented and, in 1869, five Cambridge men gave lectures to the first students. By 1872 the Hitchin house was too small and the lease was about to expire. Some of her collaborators wished to move the college to Cambridge, but Emily Davies strongly opposed this because she was anxious to avoid any possibility of scandal.

A compromise was reached when it was decided to build about two miles from the town. It was felt that this site would be near enough for visiting lecturers, but sufficiently far away from the male students. One wing and a small Hall were built in 1873. 22 of the 34 University professors admitted Girton students to their lecture-rooms, but many lectures took place at the college. A few resident female lecturers taught in the mornings, and male dons in the afternoons. In 1880 a Girton girl was placed equal to the eighth Wrangler, and in the following year women were allowed to take the Previous and Tripos Examinations.

Newnham, the second women's college, also had a very modest beginning. In October 1871, five students supervised by Anne Jemima Clough began to occupy a house in Regent Street, until Merton Hall was leased as a centre for both resident and local students. In 1874 the Lectures Association formed a limited liability company, and the building now called Old Hall was opened in 1875. The Newnham College Association was formed in 1880, and Sidgwick Hall was built. One of the early pupils, Mrs. F. A. Keynes, has said that 'The desire of our Principal, Miss Clough, . . . was that we should be as inconspicuous as possible not only in behaviour but also in appearance, in order not to alarm the doubters'. Although skirts reached almost to the ground, hockey was played on a secluded pitch, and when a visiting team brought a man as umpire, he was requested to leave.

The chaperon system survived for many years, and when Mrs. Keynes' husband went to coach a Girton student in the mid-seventies, the Mistress remained in the room, busily knitting, to watch over his pupil, although the girl was senior to himself. A lecturer in mathematics who received a letter to ask him to admit a female student to his lectures, forwarded it to the Head of his college and received it back endorsed, 'No modest female would prefer such a request'.

Until 1869 every member of the University had to belong to a college, but henceforth unattached students were admitted under the control of a Censor. Fitzwilliam Hall was assigned to them in 1893. Local Examinations for grammar school boys were established in 1858, and in 1873 a joint Oxford and Cambridge Board began to examine public school boys. Lectures given to men and women in northern towns in 1867 were so popular that the University began to organise extramural lectures. In 1927 the Board of Extra-Mural studies acquired a fine headquarters when Stuart House was opened in Mill Lane. Cavendish College, for younger and poorer students, was founded in 1873, but closed about 20 years later owing to financial difficulties. The buildings were taken over for training teachers, and the college was renamed Homerton.

In 1873, King's became the first college to admit only candidates for honours degrees. The Royal Commission on scientific instruction of 1873 reported that most of the college posts could not be retained if a man married; that only 120 of the 350 Fellows resided in Cambridge and performed teaching or administrative tasks, and that the non-resident Fellows received a large part of the income of the colleges. It suggested that the more eminent of the college lecturers should have a recognised place in the University, and that their lectures should be open to all. Another Commission found that many colleges had an income in excess of what was needed for educational purposes. An

Act of 1877 required the colleges to make contributions to University funds, and Fellows had to hold a University post.

Parliament appointed Statutory Commissioners to carry out the provisions of the Act, and revised statutes came into force in 1882. A few colleges had allowed married men to retain Fellowships, but the ban was not completely relaxed until these new statutes provided that Fellows need no longer be in holy orders nor remain celibate. Many young dons hastily found brides, who were introduced to local society at formal dinner parties at which it was customary for them to wear their wedding dress. Until the statutes of 1882, the main qualification for a Fellowship had been distinction in the University examinations, and men who excelled in mathematics, or to a lesser extent classics, had a great advantage. A Fellow who was willing to be ordained and who did not marry could retain his post although he did not teach or even reside in Cambridge. Under the new regulations, Fellows were elected for an initial period of six years, and Fellowships were only normally prolonged if a man held a college or University post.

From the sixteenth century, most of the teaching had been done by the colleges, and University professors often gave no lectures. As a result of the new statutes, the colleges were no longer completely autonomous, and the University became more important. The number of professors who actually taught was increased, more University lecturers were appointed, and colleges contributed to University funds. The present co-operative system was beginning to evolve. These reforms opened up a new era, and studies became more diverse. From the 1870s, there were intercollegiate arrangements for lectures, but undergraduate teaching was still done mainly by college lecturers and private coaches until about 1900, in spite of the increased number of University lectures, and as new subjects of study were introduced, the colleges had to appoint more lecturers. Private coaches were very important, especially for mathematics, and R. R. Webb sometimes coached for 60 hours a week in addition to giving lectures. By about 1910 a majority of the men no longer went to coaches, but depended upon the college supervisors for individual guidance. Colleges had their own lecture-rooms, often using the Hall, and a few their own laboratories.

Selwyn, at first classed as a 'public hostel', and not as an 'approved foundation' until 1926, was opened in 1882 for Church of England men of moderate means. A Teachers' Training Syndicate was established in 1879 and its secretary, Oscar Browning, became principal of a day training college for teachers in 1891. Oscar Browning was a strange mixture of flashes of genius, earnestness, vitality and enthusiasm, with an element of absurdity that made him a 'character'. He entertained widely and was treasurer of the Union, the Footlights, the Music and Hockey Clubs. At a time when there was still a great gulf between dons and undergraduates, he brought them into closer contact, and he was the best-known don of his time. He acquired the first typewriter in Cambridge; it was next owned by Dr. Courtney Kenny, who typed his famous *Outline of Criminal Law* on it. Shortly before his death, he presented the machine to Miss Pate of the University Typewriting Office, where it is still preserved. A note on the lid records that it was 'seen with much interest and tried by George Eliot'.

In the 1880s, undergraduates still drank beer at breakfast. Sport afforded an outlet for energies that had previously led to much rowdiness and disorder, although when Lord Kitchener received an Honorary Degree in 1898, his carriage was dragged from the Senate House to Christ's, and there was a huge bonfire on the Market Square in the evening. The first rugby and soccer matches with Oxford were in 1872 and 1874; the first full 'blues' for these games awarded in 1884. Golf was regularly played on Coe Fen from 1873; two years later the players moved to Coldham's Common, where the town rifle range bisected the course, and golf-balls often had to be retrieved under rifle or machine-gun fire. Barnwell youths stamped stray balls into the mud, then pretended to find them and claimed a reward.

By about 1890, May Week was an important social event, and many parents of undergraduates went to the bumping races in robust rowing-boats, big barges pulled by horses, or by road in hansom-cabs or carriages. Balls were fitted on the prows of the eights after a fatal accident in the late eighties, when a man was struck in the back. In 1892, 30 boats competed in two divisions. Every year, about 10,000 people assembled on King's lawn on the evening of the day after the last race day to watch the Boat Procession. The eights, decorated with flowers, were rowed to the Mill Pool, where they were turned and taken back to

King's to be placed side by side in rows. The crew of the second boat called for three cheers for the Head of the River crew, who remained seated to drink wine from the challenge cup, while the other crews stood with uplifted oars. Every crew was similarly toasted, and a battle of flowers ended the proceedings. The last Boat Procession took place in 1892, when the Lady Margaret boat was manned by only three men dressed in mourning, and with placards reading 'Sent Down' on the empty seats. The five missing men had been rusticated for their part in a bonfire in New Court on the previous night. Sport became so important that the reputation of a college, especially from 1895 to 1914, depended largely upon the athletic abilities of its members.

From 1895, advanced students were allowed to take a B.A. degree after residing for six terms and the satisfactory completion of some research. These arrangements were altered in 1912 when 'research students' were recognised. By an Act of 1889 the University and the town began to co-operate in local government. The Senate appointed two councillors and the colleges elected four others. The University representation was later altered to two aldermen and six councillors, and many University men have since become Mayor. There were strained relations in 1891 when the Proctors arrested and imprisoned two women alleged to be prostitutes, and after an acrimonious dispute the Cambridge University and Corporation Act of 1894 provided that suspects should henceforth appear before the Borough magistrates, and the Vice-Chancellor lost his power to license theatres and other entertainments.

Towards the end of the nineteenth century the most conspicuous college Head was the Very Reverend H. M. Butler, Master of Trinity. His majestic figure and his eloquence made him an outstanding Cambridge personality. As an elderly widower he married a Girton undergraduate and had a son. This inspired someone to write:

> *The Reverend Master of Trinity*
> *In classics supreme and divinity,*
> *Said Cato had a son*
> *At a hundred and one,*
> *Then why not the Master of Trinity?*

THE TWENTIETH CENTURY

Bicycles, horse trams and motor-cars. The New
Museums. The University between two world wars.
Recent University and college buildings

The railway had defeated the stage coaches, and now bicycles, motor-cars and buses arrived to menace horse-drawn transport. In 1869 a Cambridge resident wrote that 'The great interest of the last few days has been the new velocipede from Paris. Very delightful and magical it looks, skimming along on two wheels, one before the other'. Lord Dunedin claimed that when he was at Trinity he was the first undergraduate to ride a bicycle, and from 1874 there were Oxford and Cambridge cycling races. In 1903, when a magistrate fined a man 5/– for riding a bicycle on the footpath on Sheep's Green, he said that 'There is scarcely a place in Cambridge now where pedestrians can walk with safety. Cyclists are an utterly reckless class, who don't care tuppence about other people. They are the most selfish people in the world.'

A newspaper report of May 1896 tells us that 'Considerable interest was created amongst the townspeople on Wednesday, when the Cambridge Omnibus Company began to run their new and convenient two-horse omnibuses from the railway station to the Market Hill.' There were four vehicles, 'the exterior accommodation being seven comfortable garden seats'. The Cambridge Street Tramways Company, formed in 1879, eventually had six double-deck and two single-deck cars, each pulled by a single horse. From the depot in East Road a track ran down the centre of the road via Gonville Place, Lensfield Road and Trumpington Street to the Market Square, and another line ran from the railway station to Christ's. These horse-drawn trams continued until 1914; they moved so slowly that active persons could reach the station more speedily by walking. Four-wheelers and hansom-cabs stood on the ranks, and the large 'Lion' bus, with its top-hatted driver, plied between the hotel of that name and the station. Race-horses from Newmarket often ended their days between the shafts of Cambridge hansom-cabs.

College bedmakers, wearing black bonnets and shawls, and carrying bags in which to take away scraps salvaged from the kitchens, descended from the trams. A Dean of Trinity is said to have preached a sermon on the text: 'Gather up the fragments that remain, that nothing be lost'. Some of the bedders were only employed during the terms, others throughout the year, and social workers of the period sometimes found that the husband of a college bedmaker gave up his own work when his wife obtained a permanent college post. Bedmakers and their friends did the college washing, each for 20 to 30 men. The bundles of linen were collected by handcart, and carriers took some of the laundry to be done in surrounding villages. A large proportion of Cambridge workers depended directly or indirectly on the University, but as they were needed only during the terms, they were unemployed during a large part of every year.

In 1898 the Hon. C. S. Rolls rode a motorcycle in the Corn Exchange, and he was the first man to drive a car, a 4 H.P. Peugeot, in Cambridge streets. In the same year the Automobile Club, which then had just over 300 members, held a Whitsun tour from London to Cambridge. The 17 vehicles were followed by a baggage-van and an ambulance, a steam waggon of the type then used by the G.P.O. for carrying parcels. The cars were not allowed to exceed a speed of 14 m.p.h., and took eight hours to reach Cambridge. The 'Light Blue' vehicles of the Cambridge Motor Omnibus Co. were followed in 1907 by green 'Ortona' buses travelling at a maximum speed of 12 m.p.h. For a time they were not allowed to pass through the central streets because it was feared that they might damage shop blinds. In 1909 a taxi-cab owner was fined £2 for driving at a speed dangerous to the public; it was stated that he had been travelling at from 10 to 12 m.p.h.

The Cambridge Electricity Company first supplied current in November 1892, and for the first two years it was used only for lighting during the hours of darkness. It was one of the first three in the country to use a steam turbine invented by Sir Charles Parsons, an old St. John's man, as the sole prime mover. A disused skating-rink in St. Andrew's Street was opened as a theatre in 1882, and Master Charles Chaplin and his brother Sidney played there in *Sherlock Holmes*. The New Theatre was built on the site in 1895; the inaugural performance was *Hamlet* played by the Haymarket Theatre Company headed by Mr. (later Sir Herbert) Beerbohm Tree. From the eighties, the University Penny Popular Concerts Association provided Saturday evening entertainments, arranged by each college in turn, in the Guildhall. These 'Penny Pops' continued for some years after Sturton Town Hall (now the Kinema) and the Victoria Assembly Rooms began to show films in 1910.

The colleges derived much of their income from the ownership of land, and the depression in agriculture caused receipts to fall. In 1888–93 the University was desperately short of money, colleges were unable to pay their full contributions, and an appeal had to be made to private benefactors. The salaries of professors and lecturers were so low that, in the absence of any pension schemes, many very aged dons could not afford to retire. Some people said that only state aid could remedy the situation, but many feared that this would menace the University's independence.

A Royal Commission of 1919 reported that 'The growth of science at Cambridge since the era of the Royal Commissions has been perhaps the greatest fact in the history of the University since its foundation.' A new chemical laboratory was opened in 1889, and an anatomy school in 1891. The garden of Mortlock's bank was purchased five years later, and large parts of the Downing grounds were bought between then and 1902. In the first decade of the twentieth century, many new buildings arose on both sides of Downing Street—the Sedgwick Museum of Geology, a law school and library, the Museum of Archaeology and Ethnology, buildings for agriculture, botany and physiology, and extensions to the chemical and Cavendish laboratories. In 1907 there were only five lecture-rooms for the 46 teachers of arts subjects, but the Examination Hall was opened in 1909 and new lecture-rooms in 1911. Private benefactors endowed professorships, and a business firm financed a chair of German. The first professor of Italian, Thomas Okey, appointed in 1919, had worked in his youth as a basket-maker.

Proposals that degrees should be given to women were defeated in 1888 and 1896–7. In a poll organised by the *Cambridge Review* in 1896, the undergraduates voted against the proposals 1,723 to 446, and the vote in the Senate House in 1897 was 1,707 against and 661 for. While the voting was in progress, excited crowds gathered near the Senate House and climbed on to the roof of Great St. Mary's, and undergraduates suspended a female figure on a bicycle from the upper windows of the bookshop opposite.

The outbreak of war in 1914 almost suspended all activity in the University. By 1916, only 575 of the 3,263 students remained. The colleges accommodated about 2,000 officer cadets, and my schoolboy friends found their training trenches and dugouts near the Grantchester Meadows admirable for mock battles. Thousands of soldiers were encamped on the commons, and until the First Eastern Hospital was built on the cricket ground of King's and Clare, beds for wounded men from France were placed beneath Trinity Library and in the cloisters of Nevile's Court.

After the war, government grants to ex-service students and state scholarships helped to swell the numbers of undergraduates. In 1920 there were 5,733 men below M.A. level in residence. The ex-service men were difficult to discipline, and rags were frequent. The finances of the University were severely strained, and in 1922 a Royal Commission proposed that fees for teaching should no longer be paid to colleges or to individual lecturers, but to Faculty Boards; that there should be a retiring age and a pensions scheme for teachers; and that half of the Fellowships should be held by University lecturers and demonstrators. Legislative power should be transferred from the Senate to the House of Residents, and college contributions to the University should vary according to their wealth.

A pension scheme was adopted in 1923, and a Statutory Commission of 1923–5 accepted most of the Royal Commission's proposals. A centralised secretariat was set up, and women became eligible for professorships and lectureships. The new statutes came into force in 1926. It was in this year that Terence Gray opened the derelict Theatre Royal at Barnwell as the Festival Theatre, built a new stage with a turntable and the first cyclorama in the country, and made it the most progressive theatre in England. The plays ranged from Greek drama to modern comedy, and future stars included Flora Robson, Robert Donat and Maurice Evans. Sir Tyrone Guthrie was producer for a time. From 1879 to 1915 the building had been a mission hall, and a lantern over the stage door still had 'God is Love' painted on one side, and 'All Have Sinned' on the other.

The University received very large benefactions between the two wars from commercial firms, private individuals, and other sources. The Rockefeller Foundation gave £133,000 for a Pathological

Laboratory opened in 1928. In the meantime the first part of the new Engineering Laboratory and the Institute of Biochemistry had been built. At the Cavendish Laboratory, the Royal Society Mond Laboratory was opened in 1932, and a gift from Lord Austin enabled a new wing to be put up. Most of the new developments were for branches of science, but in 1933 the literary faculties gained a new block of lecture-rooms in Mill Lane. Another munificent Rockefeller gift of £700,000 was partly used for a new University Library and a building for zoology. When the Library was opened in 1934, the former buildings were adapted for University offices and reception rooms, and for the history, law and other libraries. A new School of Anatomy was opened in 1938.

During the Second World War there were still many undergraduates in residence, and about 2,000 students evacuated from London. A number of government departments and cadet forces occupied some of the college buildings, and Sir Will Spens, Master of Corpus, was Regional Commissioner for the Eastern Region throughout the war. With the exception of the Union, air-raid damage to University and college buildings was negligible. After the war, students flocked to the University; the number increased from 5,374 in 1938–9 to 7,016 in 1954–5. For many years most of the undergraduates were older than pre-war students, since a large proportion did National Service before they came up. Women at last acquired equal status in 1947, and when the Queen Mother received an Honorary Degree, she became the first Cambridge woman graduate. A third college for women, New Hall, opened in temporary accommodation in 1954.

Since the war, many new buildings have been constructed. The Downing site was fully occupied by 1939, and the Veterinary School opened in 1955 in Madingley Road, where Churchill College occupies a large site. The Engineering Laboratory has been greatly enlarged, a new Chemical Laboratory built in Lensfield Road, and for the Arts Faculties there are several big blocks in Sidgwick Avenue. Many colleges have constructed additional buildings, some, like Christ's, Peterhouse and Queens', within their boundaries, but others have built further away. King's and Caius have put up blocks of chambers in West Road, Clare in Chesterton Road, and Emmanuel in Newmarket Road. Fitzwilliam House opened its new buildings in Huntingdon Road in 1963, and New Hall is nearing completion on an adjoining site.

II

The Present

UNTIL COMPARATIVELY recent times, during the Long Vacation from June until September, Cambridge became a quiet market town. The undergraduates departed and a large proportion of the college servants were paid off, some to take temporary jobs as cooks or waiters at seaside hotels. Now, at least until the end of August, one notices scarcely less activity in the streets. Cars bring an ever-increasing number of visitors, and many students come up for the Long Vacation Term. Coach-loads of tourists arrive from other lands, to be shepherded round half a dozen colleges by competent official guides, or by others with a superficial knowledge of history but a better acquaintance with legends and anecdotes. Hundreds of foreign girls and a smaller number of boys come to Cambridge to learn English, and one cannot walk down any of the central streets without hearing several languages being spoken. It is the time of the year, too, when one sees many people wearing discs to indicate their identity—a sign that yet another conference is being held. Academic conferences attract delegates from all over the world, and learned and professional bodies hold meetings or courses. The colleges which accommodate them are glad to earn the additional income to help to pay the wages of a permanent staff. It is not until September that there is a lull before the storm, before 9,000 young men and women, and the dons who teach them, return at the beginning of October.

British Railways lorries, piled high with trunks and bicycles, are the first sign of the coming invasion. All preparations have been made;

rooms have been redecorated, college groundsmen have marked out pitches and painted goalposts, bookshop stocks are at their peak, placards advertise secondhand gowns and cycles, and many a small newsagent displays a 'Lecture List Sold Here' notice. The academic year begins on October 1st, but 'Full Term', i.e. the period during which undergraduates keep their 59 nights, not until about a week later. On October 1st the Vice-Chancellor addresses the Congregation of the Senate, reviews the past year, indicates future trends, and invariably refers to strained finances; his speech is an annual report on the state of the University. Some of the undergraduates arrive early, particularly the freshmen, since Tutors must have time to interview them.

Almost every year, during the first weeks of the Michaelmas Term, the sun shines on the autumnal tints of the trees. It is still possible to enjoy boating on the river, to lie in a punt and gaze up at white clouds sailing across a brilliant blue sky. Cambridge is, perhaps, more beautiful then than in early Spring, when the first leaves appear in all their freshness, when thousands of crocuses and daffodils line the avenues of the Backs, and Trinity avenue is bordered by cherry-trees loaded with white blossom. Rain often curtails the tennis and cricket, the river picnics of the Summer Term, and impending examinations keep many men indoors. Even in June, May Week festivities may be held in cold and sunless weather, but in October, sunshine usually welcomes both freshmen and those who are returning to Cambridge.

The freshman enters either a large, medium or small college. St. John's has approximately 720 undergraduates and Trinity 880, while at the other end of the scale are Sidney Sussex with about 230 and Peterhouse with 250. About 800 come from the Commonwealth or the U.S.A. There are ten times as many men as women, and the latter, who always live in college, will have had to pass a more exacting test to obtain a place. The disparity between the number of men and women is somewhat alleviated because there are always a great many foreign girls in the city, girls at teachers' training colleges or in University offices, and the nurses of Addenbrooke's Hospital.

Oxford and Cambridge produce nearly a quarter of the graduates in the country. The colleges, not the University, decide who is to be admitted, and the right of a college to choose its entrants is a cherished privilege, since it helps it to retain its individual character. To obtain a place, the candidate must usually pass an examination and satisfy Fellows who interview him, and his record during the previous few years, as well as the result of the examination, is taken into account. Many people imagine that brilliant young men are denied entrance to Oxford or Cambridge because the colleges prefer to admit the mediocre sons of former members, but this is now completely untrue. Candidates are primarily selected on their academic achievement, and one proof of this is that only about 4 per cent fail to obtain a degree; at other universities over 14 per cent fail. In the past, men who were not clever could come to Cambridge to enjoy the social life or try to get a Blue, and sit for an Ordinary Degree, but today they must all read for Honours.

Most colleges have a special link with certain schools. Several of the Fellows may be old boys of them, and some scholarships have been endowed to assist boys from certain schools. A college tutor knows many headmasters, housemasters and subject masters, persons who select, encourage and prepare boys of genuine intellectual merit, and a report on a boy from a schoolmaster well known to a tutor is often a more reliable guide to his ability than an examination result. About 40 per cent of the freshmen come from grammar schools, and about 45 per cent read Natural Science and allied subjects. The popularity of the Arts subjects is declining, as there are twice as many passes at 'A' Level in Science as in the Humanities. A man with a scientific training can more easily find a job and a better chance of a good income, but at Oxford nearly two-thirds of the students still take Arts courses.

The average undergraduate works much harder than the pre-war student; a 'First' is now more important than a 'Blue', and Tripos results mean the difference between one job or another. Some people believe that the University was a happier place when status and prospects did not depend so much on academic performance, and insist that the object of a university education is not merely to prepare men to pass examinations.

Every man spends at least one year in college, and the remainder of his period of residence in hostels or in rooms which have been approved by the University Lodging House Syndicate. Some houses have been lodging students for over a century, and men who in later years become famous often keep in touch with humble Cambridge folk with whom they lodged. 11 colleges place all or almost all of their first-year men in college; five send them into lodgings, where they often feel lonely and find it more difficult to make friends. The remainder place a part of the freshmen in lodgings. In the colleges, 'Bedders' clean and tidy the rooms, and the social gulf that once existed between bedders and students has largely disappeared—in fact many of the smart and good-looking women who keep a number of rooms tidy are better off than the parents of some of the men they serve. Manservants called 'gyps' formerly looked after one or more staircases, but today most of the male staff perform the more onerous cleaning tasks, look after boilers, wait at table in Hall, or are cooks, porters or gardeners. Many of them give a lifetime of service to their college, and watch with interest the subsequent careers of men who become eminent.

College rooms are of infinite variety, ranging from the mediaeval to the contemporary. A freshman may be allotted an ancient room and discover the names of famous men who once occupied it; this may be some compensation for a small window, draughts, and poor toilet facilities. There are college rooms still in the jug and basin age, where the occupants have to wash in cold water, and where a hod of coal is left at the foot of the staircase. Other men may be the first occupants of a comfortable room in a building just completed.

A pile of literature awaits every freshman—advertisements from banks, insurance companies and shops; invitations to join a host of clubs and societies. Every undergraduate pays a subscription to the Amalgamated Clubs of his college, and this is added to his bill. He can then belong to almost all of the college clubs and societies. The treasurer is usually a don who serves as a liaison officer between the students and the staff. There are also the clubs and societies not connected with specific colleges; *Varsity Handbook* lists about 225— among them the Buddhist Society, the Lutheran Society, and the Society of King Charles the Martyr; the University Pipers, the Cambridge Anarchist Group, The Heretics, and the Guild of Change Ringers; the Mummers (a dramatic society), the Ichthyan Singers (a choir singing music ranging from Elizabethan Motets to Negro Spirituals), and the Damper Club (membership restricted to persons who have, while clothed, unwittingly fallen into the river from a punt). At the Cambridge Societies Fair, held at the beginning of the term in the Examination Hall and the Corn Exchange, over 100 organisations offer information about their activities, and as a writer in *Varsity Handbook* said, 'There is no compulsion to join anything, but three years' blinkered study may well cause future regret'.

The freshman has to note University and college rules, learn that gowns must be worn at lectures, in libraries and chapels, when calling upon Tutors and supervisors, and in the streets after dusk. 'Squares', known elsewhere as 'mortar-boards', were abandoned during the Second World War. Most men acquire secondhand gowns from outfitters or college porters, and although all gowns look much alike, except that a M.A.'s gown is longer and some are more torn and threadbare than others, they do also differ slightly in style or in the shade of black or blue, according to the college.

Undergraduates are not allowed to keep a motor vehicle within 25 miles of Great St. Mary's church, and only B.A.s or men over 22 can normally obtain permission to have a car. Almost everyone finds that a cycle is a necessity to get to and from lectures and sports fields, and more cycles are probably to be seen in Cambridge than in any other town of equal size. In the narrow streets they are a nightmare to motorists. Child cyclists are well trained at school but can have occasional lapses, many elderly riders wobble dangerously, foreign girls are liable to make all manner of unorthodox manœuvres, and undergraduates rushing to lectures take innumerable risks. In an effort to curb the Cambridge custom of 'borrowing' the nearest bike, all cycles owned by students have a letter denoting the college and a number painted on the rear mudguard. Under a byelaw, a fine of £5 can be imposed upon anyone convicted of using a cycle without the owner's consent. The police have a large store for lost cycles; in 1962, 2,841 were found abandoned in the streets, and 2,062 were restored to their owners.

Dinner in Hall is a survival from the communal life of the monasteries, and at most colleges, two sittings have to be held. Two or three rows of tables, without tablecloths, and with benches on each side, extend down the length of the Hall, while the dons dine at the High Table on a dais at a higher level. There are occasional complaints about the food; an entry in one Junior Common Room suggestions book read: 'Last night's jugged hare was evidently dug up, not shot', and in a college where the diners eat by candlelight it is alleged that the dimness is intentional, so that men cannot see what they are eating.

Meals in Hall provide the freshman with an opportunity to observe the dons, some of them world-famous. Many have become more widely known than their predecessors, some only to devotees of the Third Programme, but others, through television, are almost as familiar to the multitudes as film stars. Dons may sit on Royal Commissions and give their names to Reports, or are consulted by the Government. The growth of the applied sciences, with their numerous specialised sub-divisions, has led to a very great increase in the number of teachers and administrators, many of whom cannot be given Fellowships. Efforts are made to absorb them into the college system by offering them dining rights, but High Tables can only accommodate a limited number. Some of the dons, too, who spend most of their time in a laboratory, have little desire to participate in college life. Fellows work in co-operation to administer estates, to house, feed, advise and teach undergraduates and research students, and even if it were possible to increase the number of Fellows, many of them could only play a small part in the working life of their college.

For some time there has been a need for a centre where all senior members and graduate students can meet to entertain their wives or guests, a place where the University can welcome scholars and other important visitors or hold conferences. A gift of £330,000 from the Wolfson Foundation will enable the University to provide for this need on a site beside the river at the bottom of Mill Lane. There are today only a few celibate Fellows who spend most of their life in college. A resident Fellow is normally provided rent-free with a study, dining-room and bedroom, and does not pay for heating, lighting, service and his Hall dinners. Eccentric dons are less numerous than in former times, although on several occasions I have noticed one trimming the hedge of the Fellows' Garden with a small pair of secateurs. As the hedge is 100 yards long and six feet high, he has plenty of scope to continue his snipping indefinitely.

Professors were once majestic figures in cap and gown, but except on special occasions they are now more likely to be seen in sports jackets and flannel trousers. Most of the college Masters are elected by the Fellows, who occasionally choose a man who has had a distinguished, though not an academic career, like Field-Marshal Sir William Birdwood, Sir Henry Willink or Sir Frank Lee. The Master of Trinity is appointed by the Crown. A Master's wife often has to cope with an enormous Lodge designed to be run by at least half a dozen servants, but now she, perhaps, has only a couple of foreign girls who require time off every day to go to English lessons.

The Chancellor is elected for life, and this mainly honorary position has been occupied in modern times by Lord Balfour, Earl Baldwin, and Lord Tedder. The Chancellor may only be seen publicly in Cambridge in June, when he awards honorary degrees. The Vice-Chancellor is elected annually by the Senate, but serves for two years. On important occasions he wears the only mediaeval cope still in use. All of the 60,000 to 70,000 M.A.s, many living in remote parts of the world, are members of the Senate, and the Council of the Senate is in effect the University cabinet. It frames rules and proposes action, and suggests Graces, to which assent is given by a 'placet', meaning that the members of the Senate accept the recommendation. If there are objections, notice of a 'non-placet' is given, and both the dissidents and the promoters issue fly-sheets to state their case. Fly-sheets were produced, for instance, in 1963 when some members opposed an honorary degree for Lord Hailsham, and a proposal to build a public lavatory beside an entrance to the Botanic Garden was also attacked in a fly-sheet. The resident teaching and administrative staff, numbering over 1,400, are Members of the Regent House. The Senate votes on certain Graces, but only the Regent House on all others.

The Proctors were of great importance in former times, and they still rank next to the Vice-Chancellor, and attend him at the Senate House and at the University Sermons. The Senior and the Junior Proctors are assisted by four Pro-Proctors. When they are acting officially, they wear full academical dress, including the hood of their degree, and are accompanied by two University servants known as 'Bulldogs' or 'Bullers' who wear full morning dress with top hats. Bulldogs attending a Proctor at the Senate House or Great St. Mary's wear blue cloaks and carry a linstock, a partizan or short pike, and a volume of the statutes.

Proctors maintain discipline, grant permission for dinners and dances, and keep an eye on undergraduate magazines. Proctorial permission is required for a dinner or a party at an hotel or public room if more than 15 persons are to be present, also for any dance or club meeting held outside a college. Accompanied by their 'Bullers' they parade the streets after dark, watching for gownless students. A 'Buller' may suddenly accost a likely victim to ask him whether he is a member of the University. If he is, he is requested to speak to the Proctor. The Proctor gravely lifts his square, asks the man his name and college, records them in a notebook, lifts his square once again and moves away. On the following morning the culprit receives a note, asking him to call upon the Proctor, and he will have to pay a fine of 6/8d., equivalent to half a mediaeval mark.

The Proctors sometimes enter public-houses, cinemas and dance-halls. They cannot pursue a man who has reached the sanctuary of his college, nor do the police ever enter a college unless invited to do so by a Tutor. For offences too serious to be dealt with by a fine, a man may be 'rusticated', i.e. obliged to leave Cambridge for a time, and then must make up the lost period at the end of his period of residence, or he is 'sent down' or expelled. The most severe penalty is only inflicted for a very serious offence, and the decision is taken by the governing body of the man's college.

On special occasions, when the Chancellor or Vice-Chancellor walk in procession, they are preceded by two Esquire Bedells who carry maces. An Esquire Bedell is first mentioned in 1473; the early occupants of the office were 'privileged persons' but not members of the University. There were originally three, but one was abolished in the middle of the nineteenth century. They now have only ceremonial functions, and are senior members.

The Council of the Senate consists of the Chancellor, who rarely comes to Cambridge, the Vice-Chancellor and 16 graduates chosen by the Regent House. It examines all Graces and nominates persons to serve on other University bodies. The Secretary of the Council, named the Registrary, supervises records of University affairs and edits the *University Reporter,* the official gazette. A Financial Board consisting of the Vice-Chancellor and 10 members of the Senate controls properties, the income and expenditure of the University, and publishes the annual accounts of the University and the colleges; its secretary is the University Treasurer. The General Board of Faculties considers the arrangements for teaching and lecturing proposed by the Faculties, and appoints examiners.

About a score of Faculty Boards make recommendations to the General Board, and there are many other Boards and Syndicates to administer Local Examinations, Extra-Mural Studies, the University Library, the University Press, the Botanic Garden, etc. All of these bodies can initiate University legislation by submitting reports and recommendations for the approval of the Council of the Senate. Many dons not only help to govern their own college but also serve on University committees.

Among the occupants of the High Table are the Tutors, Bursar, Dean, Steward, Praelector, Librarian and Lecturers. In the Cambridge college system, a Tutor occupies a very important place. He advises undergraduates about their studies, and is available to assist them in personal problems. Most colleges have several Tutors. Bursars administer estates and investments and control the servants. Agricultural rents were at one time almost the only source of income, but now that colleges own a wide variety of property, and shares in public companies, the work of a Bursar has become far more onerous, and he needs a staff. Some colleges are far more richly endowed than others. The Dean, normally a Fellow and a clergyman, is responsible for Chapel services, but some colleges have a 'Dean of College' who is responsible for discipline within the college. Stewards supervise the Hall and kitchens. Today, the only duty of a Praelector or Father of the college is to ensure that a student has kept his terms and passed his examination before he presents him to the Vice-Chancellor for the award of his degree.

Undergraduates are taught in lectures and classes arranged by University Faculties, and in supervisions arranged by the colleges. Attendance at lectures is not obligatory, and some of the more immature students do not readily adapt themselves to a system which leaves a man so much to himself. Some people think that the invention of printing made lectures an anachronism long ago, while others assert that a good lecture can give life to a subject, indicate aspects to be explored, and present the student with ideas to ponder. A few brilliant lecturers can retain packed audiences, but some eminent scholars

are dull lecturers, too factual, lifeless, or inaudible. Freshmen believe that they should go to a great many lectures, and during the first few weeks of the Michaelmas Term, at about 9, 10, 11, 12 and 1 o'clock, certain streets are crammed with young men and women rushing from one lecture to another on cycles. As the academic year advances, some men find that they can more profitably spend their time in libraries, and the mad rush around every hour noticeably diminishes.

Directors of Studies arrange for each student to be allocated to one or more supervisors, who may not be a member of the same college, or even of the University. Many teaching officers are reluctant to supervise because it is not well paid, or because their time is occupied by college offices or research, and an increasing part has to be done by people who are not Fellows or lecturers. The subjects for study have become so diverse that even a large college like St. John's, with over 70 Fellows, cannot from its own staff provide enough supervisors in all subjects. For his supervisor, the student writes a weekly essay, which is discussed when they meet for an hour. In a supervision, one or at most two men read their essay. In the subsequent discussion, they may discover that although it was not too difficult to set down some ideas, it is not so easy to defend them when they are challenged.

The success of the system depends not only on the calibre and enthusiasm of the supervisor, but also on the ability and industry of the student. If a man has read adequately and thought about what he has learned, a supervison can be interesting and valuable for both pupil and teacher. Some dons complain that undergraduates regard a supervision as another lesson, as extra coaching for the Tripos, that men do not always realise that they are not simply receptacles into which knowledge is poured; that if they do not work with concentration and application no amount of teaching can help them.

The Cambridge permissive system is designed to encourage the student to think for himself, while tutorials and supervisions prevent him from straying too far into byways, and give him the stimulus of intimate contact with a supposedly brilliant adult. To a large extent, however, a Cambridge man gains much of his education from his fellow-undergraduates, men of diverse backgrounds and interests, living together in a single community, from the friends he makes in college, labs, lecture-rooms, clubs and societies. Every college has a

Junior Combination Room, or J.C.R., where men may meet, and societies can hold their meetings.

Perhaps the best-known club is the Union, which has a dining-room, library, billiard-room and other facilities. Many famous people, and undergraduates who may one day be equally well known, speak at its Tuesday evening debates, but interest has recently somewhat declined. Women were not admitted to membership until 1963, although their claims were being discussed half a century ago. Some students join one of a number of dramatic societies, others write for or help to produce magazines. *Varsity*, a weekly newspaper, is the most professional journal of its kind entirely produced by amateur journalists. Every college has its own playing fields, and as there are no lectures between 1 and 5 p.m., a large proportion of the undergraduates take part in sport.

By Guy Fawkes Day, the freshman will have begun to settle down. Nowadays it is most unlikely that he will take any part in the observance of this day, but undergraduates formerly flocked to the Market Square in the evening to light bonfires, discharge fireworks, and attempt to extinguish the lamps. On one occasion just after the war, dynamite broke windows in the Senate House. There was often damage to property, not all due to students, and in recent years the police and the University authorities have taken strong measures to prevent hooliganism. On the evening of November 5, students are forbidden to enter the central area.

The rags of former times have completely ceased, but many people will remember some of them—the Pavement Club, when at midday on a Saturday, hundreds of undergraduates sat down in King's Parade, or the opening of Tutankamen's tomb, when a number of curious objects were brought forth from a public convenience on the Market Square. There are still occasional mock funerals, when a man who has been sent down is conveyed to the station in a coffin, and suitably attired mourners carry wreaths, while a band plays solemn music.

The spontaneous and often highly original rags of former times have given way to an organised annual event, 'Poppy Day', held on the Saturday nearest to November 11th, when a multitude of students and spectators completely disrupt normal life. Traction engines and ingenious tableaux on large lorries crawl through dense crowds in the central streets. Thousands of people wear fancy dress, there are stalls and stunts, jazz bands and the University Pipers, mock battles of strange craft on the river, cabarets and barbecues. From early morning, when toll-gates are established on roads leading into Cambridge and under-graduates breakfast on traffic islands on which they have placed a table and chairs, until midnight when the last rockets shoot into the sky, it has been a day of noise, confusion, fantasy and humour, and over £10,000 will have been collected for Earl Haig's Fund.

At the end of the first week in December, the students leave for the Christmas vacation, and about 2,000 schoolboys arrive to sit for college scholarship examinations. On Christmas Eve there is the famous Service of Nine Lessons and Carols from King's College Chapel which has been broadcast for many years. A part of the congregation will have been invited by the college, but some seats are available for others, and in the queue that forms hours before the service there are often people who have come specially from abroad. Then Boxing Day, the one day in the year when most of the colleges are closed to the public in order to preserve rights of way.

Cambridge in winter is one of the coldest places in Great Britain. There are no sheltering hills, no higher ground between the city and the Ural Mountains. Visitors from reputedly colder countries complain about the peculiar Cambridge brand, a damp cold that penetrates. I knew one foreign professor who always wore a 'smog-mask' out-of-doors in winter. But there are compensations. After snow or a severe frost, the Backs are like fairyland, the weeping willows beside the river assume a new beauty, and the ice on the river may be sufficiently thick to bear skaters. For many weeks of the Lent Term during the hard winter of 1963, when no rugger, soccer or hockey could be played and the Lent Boat Races had to be cancelled, skating was one of the few remaining forms of exercise, and hundreds of people displayed varying degrees of expertise on the frozen river.

Rowing men in training sit together in Hall and have a special diet. Crews preparing for the races are coached by dons who bawl through megaphones as they cycle along the towpath. Each college has its boathouse, and not barges as formerly at Oxford. The Lent Races are important, although they do not attract such large crowds as those held in June. The modest width of the river does not permit crews to race abreast, so the eights start one behind the other, and attempt to overhaul and bump the boat in front. A vanquished crew must immediately pull to the bank to allow other crews to pass, and on the following afternoon the winning boats start ahead of those defeated. Racing takes place on four days, and crews making bumps on every day gain their oars; most men have the date and names of the crew painted on the blade, which becomes a treasured possession. Knock-out competitions called 'Cuppers' are played between college football teams during the term, and the final matches take place amid great excitement. Enthusiastic supporters from the colleges involved form processions headed by bands to march to the ground, and seek to decorate the goal-posts with their colours.

The undergraduates depart for another vacation, groundsmen take down goal-posts and begin to prepare the turf for tennis and cricket. Hundreds of punts and canoes are repaired and painted in readiness for summer boating, but for some students the diversions of the Summer Term are somewhat overshadowed by impending examinations. There are no lectures on Ascension Day, and the choir of St. John's sing on top of the Chapel tower; Whit Monday, on the other hand, is not a holiday for the University. As the term advances, more and more visitors come to see the colleges and to lie upon the grassy banks of the river. To some extent they disturb the peace of the more popular colleges, but the authorities are very tolerant.

The examination of thousands of students necessitates complicated arrangements. There are 19 Tripos Examinations, many divided into two parts. Candidates for an honours degree must take two parts, but not necessarily in the same Tripos. Examinations take place in the Examination Hall, the Senate House and other University buildings, as well as in the Guildhall and smaller public halls. The first examinations begin in mid-term, and the students who sit for these can then look forward to several carefree weeks, provided that they are not too apprehensive about the results. The release from tension always results in a number of escapades. Two female window-dressers' dummies were once placed high on buildings, but perhaps the most notable exploit was revealed early one morning when it was seen that an Austin Seven van had been raised to the roof of the Senate House, 85 feet above the ground, during the night. The anonymous perpetrators of this remarkable feat explained that they had dismantled some scaffolding on a nearby building, and had constructed a swinging derrick to hoist the van to the roof. Then, undetected, they put back the scaffolding. The whole operation took three-and-a-half hours, and it took quite as long to get the vehicle down. A first attempt, made by 10 Civil Defence men, was abandoned after two hours, and on the following day the van had to be cut up on the roof and lowered to the ground in sections. In 1963 an Austin car, believed to have been taken up the river on four punts, was slung beneath the Bridge of Sighs during the night.

The May Races take place during the last week of term, which is always in early June. The discharge of a gun announces to the spectators that a race has begun. Soon one hears shouting in the distance, and as the sounds come nearer, one waits for the first boat to appear round a bend in the river. Within a few moments the leading crews are passing, cheered on by people running or cycling along the towpath. If their own college seems about to register a bump, elderly dons may join the people who are keeping pace with the boats.

The Chancellor confers Honorary Degrees on eminent men and women. A colourful procession moves slowly round the lawn and enters the Senate House, where the Public Orator extols the virtues of the recipients in Latin. The University occasionally honours quite humble folk who have given long service. In 1950, Miss Pate, who directed the University Typewriting Office for more than half a century, became the first local woman to be given an Honorary Degree, and more recently a stonemason's lifetime of work on college buildings was similarly recognised.

It is on an evening in May Week that the Madrigal Society concert attracts an audience of many thousands to the river near Trinity Library. The singers and many of the listeners sit in punts, others on the sloping banks. Some watch and listen from the bridge, and an adventurous few from the roof of the Library. Ducks, disorientated by this sudden invasion of their kingdom, sometimes fly overhead. The most magical moment comes at the end of the concert, when a passage is cleared in the centre of the river, and the singers' punts, illuminated by lanterns, drift slowly away in the twilight while 'Draw on Sweet Night' sounds ever more faintly.

There are numerous college concerts, plays in the open-air setting of courts or gardens, and a few balls, though the majority of these are held on the first three days of the following week. Early in the afternoon, the man who sells buttonholes takes up a position near the Senate House. The balls are held in Halls or in large marquees lined with coloured hangings and decorated with shrubs and flowers. Four to five thousand people attend the balls on a single night, to dance while most of the inhabitants of Cambridge are asleep—except on a night in 1962 when a firework display as noisy as an air-raid awakened half the population. At Trinity, the cloisters below the Library are transformed into a ballroom, and a dance-floor is laid over the stones which in places have sunk to make the surface as uneven as the floor of St. Mark's in Venice. Adjoining cloisters are carpeted, there are armchairs and settees for those who wish to sit out, and a long buffet. In 1963, Trinity sold 900 double tickets, each costing $6\frac{1}{2}$ guineas, to guests who could dance to four bands and drink free champagne.

College buildings and bridges are floodlit, trees and flowers illuminated. The night may be cold, so braziers are provided on the lawns. A photograph of the guests is taken just before dawn, then it will soon be time to set off in punts for breakfast at Grantchester. Midway through the following morning, many people in evening dress can still be seen in the streets. The Free Foresters oppose the University Cricket Club at Fenners, and the Footlights play at the Arts Theatre. This famous society was founded over 80 years ago, and there may now be one or two females in the small cast. When in 1932 women were included for the first time, the experiment was not successful, and the following year's show was called 'No More Women'. Stars who first appeared with the Footlights include Jack and Claude Hulbert, Jimmy Edwards, Kenneth Horne, Richard Murdoch, Jonathan Routh, Julian Slade and Jonathan Miller, so it is not surprising that the show is normally transferred to a London theatre for a season.

The character of May Week has changed within living memory. Few visitors now stay for a week, although every hotel room is booked months in advance. Most girl friends arrive by an afternoon train, change into evening finery in somebody's room, and depart again on the following day.

Some of the examination results are not announced until ten days after the end of Full Term, and many undergraduates stay up until the lists for their Tripos have been posted up outside the Senate House. Crowds flock to scan the notice-boards, not only students looking for their own name and those of their friends, but lecturers and supervisors curious to know how their students have fared. Senior Tutors send telegrams and letters to men who have gone down.

Successful candidates are awarded their degrees at a General Admission held on a Friday and Saturday near the end of June. They enter the Senate House according to the year of foundation of their college, those from the oldest college first. The recipients of degrees wear dark suits and fur-trimmed hoods, most of the latter hired for a few hours from an outfitter, since unless they intend to become schoolmasters or clergymen, they will never wear them again. From their college they walk headed by the Praelector, or Father of the college, and proceed four abreast towards the Vice-Chancellor. The four men in the front rank grasp a finger of the Praelector, who, raising his square, presents them to the Vice-Chancellor, and the men kneel in turn while the Vice-Chancellor speaks a Latin formula to admit them to their degree. The student then rises, bows, and goes out on to the lawn, to be greeted and photographed by admiring relatives and friends. On payment of a fee of £5, an M.A. degree may be taken three or four years later without further examination.

A man who has gained a very good degree may be urged not to go into business or a profession, but to remain at the University to do a period of research for a Ph.D., and his college may later award a research Fellowship to him. Later still, if he wishes to pursue an academic career, he may be invited by a Faculty Board to lecture, and a University appointment and a full Fellowship may eventually follow. An increasing number of post-graduates from other universities now come to Cambridge, and the University education is more and more planned to produce Ph.Ds. To gain this degree, a man has to write a thesis, often on a subject that looks alarming to the non-specialist, e.g. 'Acid-catalysed hydrogen exchange of methylpyridines and interpolation of infrared spectra of polycyclic heteroaromatics', or 'Izz Al-Dīn Al-Sulamī, his life and works, together with his Farvā'id Fī Tafsir Al-Qur'ān'. The existing colleges do not provide the best environment for graduate research students, who numbered 1,190 in 1962, and private lodgings are expensive and difficult to find. A number of colleges have therefore combined to form Darwin College, intended only for seniors.

Many undergraduates seek the assistance of the University Appointments Board, which has several secretaries with special knowledge of careers in various fields, and large firms send representatives to Cambridge to tell students about the prospects for employment. Scientists are in great demand and have a wide choice, but it is more difficult for the arts men who often have no notion of what they wish to do; these men are advised to approach the Board during their second year.

During the vacations, and particularly in the Long Vacation, most undergraduates take temporary employment of all kinds. Some may help to run holiday camps, and linguists may act as couriers for Continental tours. Others combine work and play by organising expeditions to remote parts of the world.

III

Perambulation

*The itinerary adopted is circular, or rather elliptical. It is
necessarily selective, and describes only what an energetic visitor
could see in one day. It would be preferable, however, to devote
several days to it. The more leisured visitor might notice many
unusual or beautiful things not mentioned in the following
pages—fine ironwork of gates, railings and ancient lanterns;
murderous spikes and broken glass surmounting college walls.
Most visitors see Cambridge by day, but when darkness has fallen
and the windows of Halls and Chapels glow with colour, the
dimly-lit courts assume a new beauty.*

WE WILL begin our perambulation in Bene't Street, near the city
centre, for here is the oldest building in the county and the best
remaining example of a small mediaeval college court. The oldest
building, the Anglo-Saxon tower of **St. Bene't's** church, was already
standing when William the Conquerer landed. The narrow nave, no
wider than the tower, had no aisles until they were added in about
1300. They were rebuilt and widened in the nineteenth century.
Inside the church, the tower arch is completely preserved. A seven-
teenth- or eighteenth-century fire-hook kept in the church is a reminder
of the days when fire-hooks fastened to long poles were used to drag
down blazing thatch, and old houses often had iron rings on the eaves,
through which ropes were passed to support the weight of the hook
and pole. Thomas Hobson was buried in the chancel in 1632, and
Fabian Steadman, the inventor of change-ringing, was parish clerk in
about 1650. On the opposite side of the road is the Eagle Hotel, an
old coaching inn with a gallery in the yard.

From Free School Lane, to the east of the church, one can see the
well-preserved outer north wall of the Old Court of **Corpus**, built of
stone rubble and clunch over 600 years ago, and a narrow gallery of
two storeys which gave access to the church from the college. The

vaulted archway beneath the upper gallery was the original approach to Corpus. The Old Court, reached through a narrow passage to the west of the church, is the earliest surviving enclosed Court. The mid-fourteenth-century buildings have been altered and restored, but they give a remarkably good idea of a mediaeval college. Here, in this small quadrangle, were the Hall, Butteries, Kitchen, Master's Lodge and three rows of chambers. The old Hall is now a kitchen. The buttresses were added when the walls began to give way, garrets were built in the sixteenth century and most of the windows have been altered. A modern window in the north-west corner commemorates Marlowe and Fletcher.

The students worshipped in St. Bene't's church until Dr. Cosyn, Master from 1487 to 1515, erected a two-storeyed building, with a chapel on each floor, on the south side of the chancel; the lower chapel is now a vestry. A college Chapel was begun in 1579, and this was demolished when New Court was built in 1823–7 to the plans of William Wilkins. The architect considered this to be his best work in the Gothic style, and in accordance with his wishes, was buried in the new Chapel. The Hall, on an upper floor on the north side of New Court, has an open timber roof, linenfold panelling, the Royal Arms on the wall behind the dais, and fine armorial glass. Matthew Parker was admitted to Corpus in 1533, and later appointed chaplain to Anne Boleyn. He became Master in 1544, Dean of Lincoln in 1552, and in the reign of Queen Mary had to flee to Frankfurt because he supported Lady Jane Grey, but on the accession of Queen Elizabeth he became Archbishop of Canterbury. In 1648 his body was exhumed from his grave at Lambeth, and buried beneath a dunghill; it was re-interred at Lambeth after the Restoration. The Library at Corpus contains treasures assembled by Archbishop Parker after the Dissolution of the monasteries, and is one of the most important collections of manuscripts and early printed books in the country. There is a sixth-century Canterbury Gospels believed to have belonged to St. Augustine, the best MS of the Anglo-Saxon Chronicle, an illuminated Bible that has been called 'probably the finest English book of the twelfth century', and books printed by Caxton and Siberch. When the Archbishop gave this unique collection to his old college he stipulated that it should be kept under three locks, the keys to be held by the Master and two Fellows; the

books and MSS were to be inspected annually by the Masters of Gonville and Caius and of Trinity Hall, and should more than a certain
number of the books be missing, the collection would be forfeited
to Caius. This scrutiny has been carried out for nearly four centuries.

St. Catharine's, across the road, is now-reorientated, as in earlier
times the entrance was in Queens' Lane. Between pleasing twentieth-
century blocks that harmonise well with the older buildings, we see
the Principal Court built of brick that has weathered well and which,
in certain lights, has a violet tinge. It is fortunate that a contemplated
east range to make a closed court was never built, as the height of the
buildings would have been too great for the space enclosed. Fuller
says that 'Indeed this house was long town-bound (which hindered the
growth thereof) till Dr. Goslin that good physician cured it of that
disease, by giving the Bull Inn thereto'. Goslin was a Master of Caius,
and it is said that in former times the Fellows of his college were
accustomed to drink 'to the unhappy memory of Dr. Gosling, who
was such a goose as to leave the Bull to Catherine'. Rebuilt as the Bull
Hotel, it is now part of the college.

By 1673 the early buildings on a restricted site were in bad condition,
and it was decided to demolish all except the range to the north in
Queens' Lane. The Hall and the west and south ranges were completed by 1695. The Hall was altered by Fawcett in 1868-9, when he
inserted Gothic windows, added a large oriel, and remodelled the
interior. Additional dining space was gained in 1932 when the Combination Room above the Buttery and Screens was opened up towards
the Hall. Houses once stood between Trumpington Street and the
college, while the stables of the George Inn, occupied by Thomas
Hobson, extended as far as the west wall of the Chapel. This building,
begun in 1703 by Robert Grumbold, the mason for the ranges rebuilt
a few years earlier, has an interesting east front with motifs from the
Wren Chapel of Pembroke. The interior has a plain ceiling with a
decorated cornice, and a fine reredos carved by John Austin. In 1756
the Library was placed above the Hall, and in 1757 the Ramsden
Building designed by James Essex continued the south range in the
style of the earlier work.

The forecourt was cleared and planted with elms, and the lawn laid
out with a flower garden in the middle, still in existence in 1814, 'a

small but pretty spot, and kept very neat, and on a Pedestal in the Centre stood a Statue of Charity, with a child at her breast, and two more by her side'. The ancient elms became dangerous and had to be cut down in 1921. To provide part of a site for the Master's Lodge by Fawcett (1875–6), nine dwelling-houses built only about 40 years earlier were demolished. The Lodge is based upon the Elizabethan brick and stone style of Sawston Hall, and like other Victorian Lodges it is very large. The site could have been used more profitably for a new court. In about 1880 St. Catharine's was under a cloud but King's was flourishing; an amalgamation was proposed, but the idea was finally abandoned.

When a new Master had to be chosen in 1861 there were five electors, two of whom, Robinson and Jameson, were candidates. Jameson voted for Robinson and the latter for himself; he was entitled to do so, as it had been the college custom for candidates to vote for themselves. Of the other three electors, two voted for Jameson and one for Robinson, thus the latter gained the Mastership by three votes to two. Jameson did not at first appear to be dissatisfied, but for reasons still obscure his feelings towards his rival changed to bitter hatred; he broke his Fellow's oath of secrecy and broadcast his grievance throughout the University. He gained the sympathy of many dons, and the whole college was 'sent to Coventry' for almost half a century, until Robinson died in 1909. The controversy deterred students from seeking to enter St. Catharine's, and in five years between 1864 and 1877 there were only 11 freshmen annually. Later Masters and Tutors have long since re-established the reputation of the college.

If we turn to the right on leaving St. Catharine's we pass **St. Botolph's.** There was a twelfth-century church here, but the nave and aisles were rebuilt in the first half of the fourteenth century, the attractive tower in the fifteenth. Botolph Lane contains a delightful group of small cottages. To the right is the Pitt Building, and then, to the left, **Pembroke.** An impression of the appearance of the early buildings can be gained by taking a few steps down Pembroke Street. The first half of the north range of Old Court was refaced in brick in 1663, but further along the ancient clunchwork is still visible. The main front towards Trumpington Street is original, but this and the old buildings within the Court were ashlar-faced in the eighteenth century. Towards the south end of the street façade is the fine west end of Wren's Chapel, with a large arched window and an octagonal lantern above a large pediment crowning the wall.

The Old Court, begun in about 1365, measured only about 90 feet by 50 feet, yet for about 250 years it provided for all the needs of the college. It was the smallest court in the University. In the north-west corner is the Old Library, formerly the Chapel licensed by the Pope in 1354, the first of the college chapels in Cambridge, with a beautiful plaster ceiling of 1690 by Henry Doogood of London who worked in more than 30 of Wren's city churches, and some bookcases of the same period. In 1879 there were plans to demolish it, but they were abandoned after strong protests from G. G. Scott. The east range, including the original Hall, Master's Lodge and the south range of chambers, were demolished in 1874–5 by Waterhouse, who then built a new Hall. In 1925 it was lengthened by taking in the Combination Room, and rooms were placed above it. Most of the elaborate exterior decoration was removed.

Beyond this is Ivy Court with north and south ranges built in the seventeenth century, and to the east a block of chambers and a garden with an ancient bowling-green. The New Building, designed by the younger G. G. Scott in 1883, is one of the best of its period. Return to First Court and cross to the Chapel built in 1663–4, the first completed work of Sir Christopher Wren and the earliest sacred building in England in a pure classical style. While he was imprisoned in the Tower of London, Dr. Matthew Wren made a vow that if it pleased the Almighty to restore him to his paternal estates, he would 'return unto Him by some holy and pious employment, that summe and more, by which of His gracious providence was unexpectedly conveyed in unto me during my eighteen years captivity . . . from sundry noble and truly pious christians'.

He was Bishop of Ely when, to fulfil this vow, he provided money to build a Chapel at Pembroke, where he had been a Fellow, and entrusted the task to his nephew, who in 1663 was a scientist and 31 years old. Architecture was then hardly a profession, and most of the earlier architects had been active in other spheres. At the same time, Christopher Wren began to build the Sheldonian Theatre at Oxford. The Chapel was lengthened in 1880 to the designs of Sir George G.

Scott, to provide a short chancel separated from the original plain rectangle by Corinthian marble columns. The original part has a very fine plaster ceiling, there are interesting seventeenth-century cushions, and the altar-piece by Barroccio once belonged to Sir Joshua Reynolds. A cloister with rooms above, built to connect the Chapel with the old south range, was consecrated for the burial of students who died in college.

Waterhouse replaced old buildings with others quite out of place in Cambridge. He built the red brick range beyond the Chapel, the Library range, Hall and Master's Lodge. He was also responsible for the destruction of the Sphere, the first planetarium, large enough to seat 30 persons, built by Roger Long, Master from 1733 to 1770, an autocratic and quarrelsome man who was Professor of Astronomy and interested in mechanical devices. When a handle was turned, the audience inside the Sphere could see 'the relative situation and successive motions of the heavenly bodies'.

Pembroke was the college of Edmund Spenser, Thomas Gray, Christopher Smart, and of William Pitt, who entered it in 1773 at the age of 15 and remained intermittently until 1780. In the following year he became an M.P., was Chancellor of the Exchequer in his 22nd year and Prime Minister when only 25.

The open conduit on both sides of Trumpington Street, an unusual feature, but a trap to unwary motorists, replaced one that ran down the centre of the street until about 1794. Across the road from Pembroke is the church of **St. Mary-the-Less,** originally called St. Peter-without-Trumpington Gate. It was built in 1340-52 to replace a twelfth-century edifice and has no aisles. Until 1632 it served as the college chapel of Peterhouse, and, as at Corpus, there is a gallery giving direct access to the college. Little St. Mary's, the usual name of the church, has a beautiful decorated east window, and near the entrance a monumental tablet of special interest to American visitors; it commemorates the Rev. Godfrey Washington (1670–1729), a former minister, and bears the family arms from which the flag of the United States was derived.

The churchyard is bounded on the south side by the fifteenth-century north wall of **Peterhouse.** Originally constructed from large blocks of clunch, and with windows of varying size and shape, it displays the alterations and renovations made throughout the centuries. Little St. Mary's Lane has some small houses which have been attractively restored. The first members of Peterhouse, the oldest college, occupied hostels on the street frontage in 1284. Adjoining Little St. Mary's is a building in the Palladian style designed by James Burrough and erected in 1738–42. The end room on the top floor was occupied by Thomas Gray, who re-entered Peterhouse in 1742. Outside the window is an iron bar to which he was prepared to fasten a rope ladder in case of fire. Fellow-students kindled a fire one night and shouted 'Fire!', whereupon Gray descended in his nightshirt. Dissatisfied with the punishment inflicted on the culprits, the poet moved across the road to Pembroke.

Burrough intended to pull down the building of 1633 with a pleasing brick oriel towards the street, but fortunately it was spared. Between these two ranges of the Outer Court is the Chapel, flanked by colonnades rebuilt in 1709. Originally built of clunch faced with brick and later with ashlar, the Chapel, begun in 1628 during the Mastership of Wren's uncle, is the most striking Cambridge building of its period. Gothic, Classical and contemporary details were combined in a remarkable way; the east end has polygonal turrets and a pediment, the west end blank arcades on the ground floor, a window flanked by niches, and a striking gable with scrolled side parts and a square-headed centrepiece. Stringent classicists are inclined to condemn it, but this unorthodox building has a distinct charm. There is a fine timber ceiling, with panels decorated with oval suns with rays, and seventeenth-century Flemish glass in the East window. The stained glass in the north and south windows was executed in rich colours by Professor Ainmüller of Munich in 1855–8.

The interior of Principal Court was ashlared by Burrough in 1728. The Hall, erected in 1286, was much restored in 1866–8 by Sir Giles Gilbert Scott, when an oriel window and some buttresses were added. The wall decorations and tiles round the fireplace are by William Morris, the glass of the oriel window by his firm. At the same time the adjoining old Parlour was enlarged to form the Combination Room, with beautiful glass designed by Burne-Jones and Ford Madox Brown. The door leading from the Screens Passage to the grove, where once there was a herd of deer, may be as early as 1290. A Library was built to the east of the Hall in 1590 when Andrew Perne, who was Master and five times Vice-Chancellor, bequeathed his fine collection of books, and money for the building. Perne changed his religious beliefs so many times that students invented a new Latin verb, *pernare*, 'to rat, turn, or change often'. The beautiful grounds, still extensive although the Fitzwilliam Museum was built on part of them, are enclosed towards Coe Fen by a wall built about 400 years ago.

The nineteenth-century Gisborne Court and the Hostel built in 1926 in a Neo-Georgian style are unremarkable, but Fen Court (1939) demonstrates that the oldest college was not afraid to erect a frankly modern building. Peterhouse too, through one of its members, Lord Kelvin, became the first college to have electric lighting throughout. The engine to drive the dynamo emitted so much smoke that the college laundresses who used Coe Fen as a drying ground were greatly inconvenienced. Peterhouse possesses the oldest college bell, made at Malines in 1548. The Master's Lodge opposite the college, built by a Fellow in 1702, has not been much altered, and is a beautiful example of the domestic architecture of the period.

Beyond Peterhouse is the **Fitzwilliam Museum,** a striking neo-Classical building in the Corinthian order begun in 1837 to the designs of George Basevi, and his most famous building outside London. Richard, seventh Viscount Fitzwilliam, left to the University the interest on a legacy of £100,000 and his pictures, engravings, illuminated MSS and books. Before the site was purchased from Peterhouse, there were proposals to build the Museum on the Bull Hotel site near St. Catharine's, on the Parade frontage of King's, in Senate House Yard, between Great St. Mary's and St. Michael's, or on the Trinity Street frontage of Caius. When Basevi died in 1845, when he fell through some scaffolding in Ely Cathedral, the building was carried on until 1847 by C. R. Cockerell, who was responsible for the impressive entrance hall. Lack of funds then caused work to be suspended. The building was completed by E. M. Barry, 1870–5. Additions in a far more subdued style have been made in the present century, and the attractive modern wing is quite unlike most other museums; further extensions were begun in 1963.

The founder's gift included paintings by Titian, Rembrandt and Veronese. Later acquisitions include many of the Dutch and Flemish

29 *The Fitzwilliam Museum (Basevi, 1837-4*

schools, early Italian paintings, and English landscape drawings and paintings. There are works by Constable, Gainsborough, Turner, Sir Joshua Reynolds, Augustus John and Stanley Spencer. Paintings by the French Impressionists include works of Renoir, Pissaro, Seurat, Degas and Matisse. There is a fine collection of armour and weapons, antiquities from Greece, Rome and Egypt, and the series of ancient Greek coins is the third in importance in the world. The Museum also has a large collection of pottery and porcelain, especially of Italian maiolica, and the Print Room contains one of the most important collections in Europe.

Fitzwilliam House, opposite the Museum, was bought in 1887 and reconstructed in 1892 to serve as a communal meeting-place for students unattached to any college. It is now used by the C.U. Graduate Society to provide a centre for graduates, their wives and husbands. In Fitzwilliam Street, Charles Kingsley lived at No. 13, and Charles Darwin at No. 22, after his voyage on the *Beagle*. The conduit erected on the Market Hill in 1614 stands since 1855 at the corner of Lensfield Road. If we turn to the right into Fen Causeway we come to the towering modern buildings of the Engineering Laboratory, and a short walk brings us to Coe Fen, and, on the other side of the bridge, Sheep's Green, where the Mill Pool is reached by the path beside the river. The vicinity of the Pool is a favourite haunt of undergraduates for drinks in the open air, and punts and canoes may be hired from boathouses on either side of the bridge for the upper or lower river. From at least Conquest times, two mills stood above the Pool—the King's Mill built by Sheriff Picot, and the Bishop's Mill belonging to the Abbot of Ely. The last mills to occupy the site were demolished in the 1930s.

A narrow way leads to **Queens'**, the college which, in the early sixteenth century, sheltered Erasmus and John Fisher, two of the most famous men in Europe. I still associate Queens' with a smell of roast beef that often emanated from a window of the kitchen when I walked along Silver Street as a child. Through the gateway flanked by towers, the third to be built in Cambridge, we enter Principal Court, built immediately after the foundation of the college in the middle of the fifteenth century. By comparison with the courts then already in existence, this was much more ambitious, and the deep red bricks used, probably imported from Holland, were so durable that the court is practically as it was built. There are square salient turrets at the external angles; Henry VI's unexecuted plans for King's envisaged similar turrets. The picturesque wall sundial was placed there in 1733, and nearby is the Old Chapel, now a reading-room, and the Library.

According to tradition, Erasmus occupied rooms for seven years at the top of the turret at the south-west angle of the court, overlooking the Mill Pool, but approached by a staircase in Pump Court. Here he no doubt worked on his famous edition of the New Testament in the original Greek, and in letters to his friends complained about the food, wine and climate of Cambridge. 'I cannot go out of doors because of the plague. . . . I am beset with thieves, and the wine is no better than vinegar. . . . I do not like the ale of this place at all. . . .My expenses here are enormous; the profits not a brass farthing. . . .'

A striking feature of the Hall is the rich coloured decorations on the roof and walls. It was built in 1449, and a flat ceiling was inserted by Burrough in 1732–4, but this was removed in 1845–6 to reveal the restored mid-fifteenth century roof; it was painted in 1875 to copy traces of the original colouring. The wood and tile decoration above the restored original fireplace is by William Morris, with figures designed by Ford Madox Brown. Morris also assisted in the painting of the roof and the stencilling of the walls.

In the second, or Cloister Court, the range on the far side with a cloister was built in about 1460. Similar cloisters to connect each end of the range with Principal Court were added in about 1495. Queens' was the first college in Cambridge to introduce cloisters, although they had been employed earlier at New College, Oxford. The picturesque building on the right, the gallery of the President's Lodge, was constructed entirely of timber and plaster in the sixteenth century with materials from the former Priory. It must then have been even more beautiful, as the three oriels rose above the roof as a complete octagon, with conical roofs surmounted by tall ornamental ironwork vanes. A large part of the range beside the river became the President's Lodge.

Pump Court is to the left of Cloister Court. Buildings of clunch and stone erected in 1564 were replaced in 1756 by the existing range designed by Essex. It is fortunate that a plan to rebuild the whole of the river frontage was abandoned, since the white brick used is not in harmony with the remainder of the college. A narrow passage in the north-east corner of Cloister Court leads to Walnut Tree Court. The buildings to the right were erected on the street frontage in 1616, and partly rebuilt after a fire in 1778. On the far side is the new Chapel designed by Bodley, with a lofty and colourful interior; it was opened in 1891, and beyond this is a late nineteenth-century range of chambers. Towards the river is the new building designed by Sir Basil Spence. This takes us into the twentieth century, yet it harmonises extremely well with the old work. Most of the ground floor has been left open to preserve a view of the Backs.

We should return to Cloister Court to cross the river by the famous wooden 'mathematical' bridge, a reconstruction of 1902 of the bridge originally erected without any nails in 1749–50. Here, as at St. John's, the college buildings rise straight out of the water. From the path to the right on the west bank we have an admirable view of the north side of the President's Gallery, and can stroll in the grove where thousands of daffodils bloom in spring. On this side of the river is a long curved building erected in 1935, and the old brewhouse and stables which were remodelled to provide two common-rooms for undergraduates.

If we turn to the right after leaving by the back gate, Newnham and Selwyn colleges and the new Arts Buildings may be reached by continuing straight ahead. To the right we have the famous 'Backs', and a short walk brings us to the rear entrance to **King's.** Just before we reach this point, we should go into the first part of West Road, where Caius have built a remarkable new hostel designed by Sir Leslie Martin, Professor of Architecture. Externally, tall brick pillars support windowless walls, and the spaces between the supports have glass doors and are used as garages. Internally, the paved court at first-floor level has rooms in three 'step-backed' storeys. The south side is left open, and a broad flight of steps leads down to the garden. The much less venturesome Garden Hostel of King's is a little further down the road on the opposite side.

We return to the Backs, where the land between the ditches of King's and Clare and Queens' Road, extending as far as Garret Hostel Lane, has belonged to King's from early times. The college also owned the similar area reaching to St. John's Wilderness, until it was sold to

Trinity in 1938. Few people realise that these two groves are college property, and that the land on both sides of the river was once a swamp. During a trial test in Trinity paddocks, river silt was found 45 feet below the present level.

The view of King's College Chapel, the Gibbs Building and the south side of Clare, seen from the Backs, is probably the finest in Cambridge. An avenue leads to the bridge erected in 1818 to replace one which was 45 yards to the north. Here we reach a wide expanse of lawn and a nearer view of the magnificent buildings beyond it. To the right are Bodley's Buildings of 1893, extended in 1935, and the former Provost's Lodge, the Library, Kitchen, and the Hall with two lanterns and a central oriel window, built soon after Wilkins had won a competition held in 1823. The large and lofty interior of the Hall is impressive, with many portraits of famous former members. Wilkins proposed to Gothicise Gibbs' Building, but lack of money prevented this.

The side of the court towards King's Parade is enclosed by Wilkins' charming Screen with Perpendicular windows, and the bulbous cupola and pinnacles of the Gatehouse. One side of this very unusual building provides a five-room dwelling for the head porter. Notice the delightful old pillar-box just outside the gate, and the varying heights and designs of the shops and houses along the Parade, which makes them such an interesting group. A Fountain, set up in 1879, stands in the centre of the court. If the college had accepted the early eighteenth-century plans of Nicholas Hawksmoor, the court would have been quite unlike what we see today. He proposed to build a momunental gateway, a Hall to the south, a cloister with a bell-tower, and a new court west of the old fifteenth-century court. For Fellows' Building he made two models which may be seen in the Chapel. Hawksmoor's plans were not adopted, and in 1723 Gibbs was appointed to design new buildings. He intended to have east and south ranges in addition to the west range, the only part actually erected. This building, in Portland stone, is one of the architect's best works, and a plainer version of Hawksmoor's second plan; it is very classical for its time. The long building is rusticated on the ground floor, and the Doric entrance gateway with an open archway has a semi-circular window above. When it was finished in 1729, no further building took place for almost a century.

The Chapel, by far the most magnificent building in Cambridge, a college chapel as large as a cathedral, was planned by Henry VI and built between 1446 and 1515. The King wished to construct a splendid edifice of such a noble form that there would be no need for elaborate ornamentation. With Eton Chapel, St. George's Chapel at Windsor, and Henry VII's Chapel at Westminster, it is one of the latest of the English Gothic structures in the high Perpendicular style. Money for building it was first derived from the revenues of the Duchy of Lancaster and confiscations of foreign priories, and later from subscriptions, the royal treasury, and gifts from Henry VII.

The parts constructed from the foundation until about 1462 are in a white magnesian limestone from Yorkshire, and the walls were then probably 60–70 feet high at the east end, but only 7–8 feet towards the west. Little progress was then made for 15 years, but work was resumed in 1476, slowly at first, but more rapidly from 1480 until the death of Richard III in 1485. The five east bays may have been roofed and occasionally used. Henry VII visited Cambridge in 1506 and decided to finish the Chapel; about 140 workmen, using an oolitic limestone from Clipsham and the Peterborough district, and from Weldon, were employed in 1508–9. The later portions were made more elaborate, the buttresses adorned with badges, supporters, etc. The master mason of the period 1508–15, John Wastell, who had worked at Canterbury, constructed the great vault, the corner turrets, the pinnacles on the buttresses, and the porches. The west window, wider than that of the east, dates from this period.

The superb interior, very long and high, has little solid wall, and most of the space is occupied by the 26 windows. The spaces between the buttresses are filled by side chapels not visible as one looks down the Chapel. Finely carved badges and emblems decorate the panels on both sides of the shafts. Notice how the crowns stand out from the walls. Above the screens of the west chapels is more heraldic carving, much more ambitious than the earlier work at the east end. One of the chief glories of the Chapel is the magnificent fan-vaulting. On each side there are 13 fans, each of 12 sections with arches. There are 62 arches in each fan, and cross-pieces with fleurs-de-lis. The total length of all of these delicate stone ribs is about two miles.

When the executors of Henry VII made contracts for the stained glass, they stipulated that it should portray 'the story of the olde lawe and of the newe lawe, after the fourme, maner, goodness, curyosytie, and clenlynes in euery poynt of the glasse wyndowes of the kynges newe Chapell at Westminster'. The first glazier was Bernard Flower, who probably made the windows for Henry VII's Chapel at the Abbey. Of the later glass painters, some were English, one came from Holland or Flanders, another was certainly a Fleming, and a third was of German extraction. The 25 great windows made in 1517–31 form the most remarkable series of that time in Europe, and York Minster is the only other great mediaeval church in England to possess all of its original glass. There are 12 tall windows with pointed two-centred arches, each of five lights, on both sides of the Chapel, and large east and west windows. In the central lights are figures known as messengers, and on either side four pictures, each filling two lights, with two above and two below the transoms. The total area of the glass is about 1,200 square yards.

Although the windows in the side chapels can easily be studied, without a guidebook it is difficult to understand what the pictures in the main windows represent, because they are too far away and the beholder is confused by the stone mullions and the leading. Most of the lower scenes are from the New Testament, in chronological order; the first six on the South side portray Gospel stories, followed by three about the Apostles. The last two depict legends about the Virgin. The upper windows do not follow such a regular sequence, but most of them are scenes from the Old Testament that correspond with the subjects beneath. The windows on the north side begin with the birth of the Virgin, followed by important events in the life of Christ, in the lower tier. The large east window depicts the Crucifixion, while the west window, completed in 1879 by Messrs. Clayton and Bell, represents the Last Judgement. The glass was removed for safety during the Second World War.

The college petitioned Henry VIII to complete the decoration, and during his reign the choir was paved with marble, the high altar, stalls, screen and rood-loft set up. The stall canopies were added in about 1675, and the black and white marble we now see replaced the original flooring in 1702. It is not known who designed the screen and choir stalls, the most magnificent wood-carving of its period north of the Alps, and the earliest large timber structure in the country completely in the Renaissance style. The cyphers H.R. and A.B. that occur in several places fix the date between 1531 and 1536, i.e. between the marriage of Anne Boleyn to Henry VIII and her execution. New doors bearing the arms of Charles I were provided in 1636. For the visit of Elizabeth I in 1564, a glazed closet was built on the loft. Thomas Dallam built an organ in 1606; the present instrument was built in 1688, but it has been reconstructed and enlarged several times, and the angels with trumpets were put up in 1859. In 1962 Rubens' magnificent painting of 'The Adoration of the Magi' was bought by Mr. Alfred Alnatt for £275,000, and presented to King's College. It is at present in the antechapel, but will eventually form the altar-piece.

A gate near the west end of the Chapel leads to Trinity Lane and the tall gateposts of **Clare**, set up in 1675, with a fine iron gate made by Warren in 1713–15. The first buildings sheltered students for only about 10 years, when, says Fuller, 'a casual fire reduced their house to ashes'. He continues, in his quaint style, 'Here, by way, whosoever shall consider in both Universities the ill contrivance of many chimneys, hollowness of hearths, shallowness of tunnels, carelessness of coals and candles, catchingness of papers, narrowness of studies, late reading and late watching of scholars, cannot but conclude, that a special Providence preserveth those places'.

Nothing remains, too, of the old court which by the middle of the sixteenth century had become ruinous. Rebuilding began in 1638, when the east range was set back considerably, and both this and the south range were finished by 1642. The gateway is fan-vaulted, and above it on the court side is a delicate semi-circular oriel of two storeys, flanked by niches, and with an ornate top storey. The Civil War caused work to be suspended until 1669, when the south half of the west range was begun, and it was finished by 1676. The influence of Wren's Chapel at Emmanuel caused the design of the river front to be drastically altered, and the master mason, Robert Grumbold, introduced giant pilasters.

The west range was left incomplete while work began on the north side, including the Hall and Kitchen, 1683–90, in a more exact Wren style, probably designed as well as built by Grumbold. The height of the building is unaltered, but there are only two storeys instead of three. In the centre of this range, the entrance to the Hall has a fine cupola. The Hall itself was remodelled internally in 1870, when the fine plaster ceiling was put up. The court was completed in 1705–15 by the construction of the north half of the west range, including the Master's Lodge, and a gateway which is much more ornate on the court side. It is remarkable that architectural unity was maintained, although the building of the court extended over 77 years; when it was finished, it looked more like a palace than a college.

The Chapel, designed by James Burrough and continued after his death by James Essex, is reached by a doorway surmounted by a large shell-hood, in the north-east corner of the court. It was built in 1763–9, and the design for the east front was clearly influenced by Wren's Chapel at Pembroke. An octagonal antechapel with a glazed lantern leads into the Chapel, which has an elliptical barrel-vaulted plaster ceiling, panelled to simulate coffering. The east end is also elliptical, with a semi-dome, richly patterned and coloured, and a painting of the Annunciation by Cipriani.

To the left of the approach to the bridge is the charming little Scholars' Garden. The bridge was built at the same time as the first range, presumably to facilitate the access of building materials, because Milne Street was very narrow. This, the oldest and the most beautiful of the college bridges, was probably designed by Thomas Grumbold. There are three spans of nearly semi-circular arches, moulded balusters of a very individual design set diagonally, and parapet rails surmounted by balls. A segment has been cut from the sixth ball on the left side.

To the right of the avenue leading to the Backs is the Fellows' Garden, then through splendid iron gates made by Warren in 1713–15 we cross Queens' Road into Memorial Court, designed by Sir Giles Gilbert Scott, built in 1924–35 and extended in 1955. The court is in a pale grey brick and in an unadventurous but very pleasing Neo-Georgian style. A large arch with a column screen forms the central feature. It is probably the most attractive work of the period in Cambridge.

Beyond Memorial Court is the new **University Library** by the same architect, constructed in 1931–4, a large steel-framed building of russet brick, 420 feet long, with a massive central tower 160 feet high, and a huge arched entrance. There are some who assert that it looks more like a factory, and the design is certainly a mixture of the traditional and the modern. The 12-storey tower is a stock-room, there are two interior courtyards, and the large reading-room at the rear is 194 feet long. The University Library is the third largest in the country, and it took eight weeks to transfer the books from the old library to the new. There are over 2½ million volumes, thousands of maps and manuscripts, and the total length of the shelving is about 45 miles. Plans for future extensions are already being considered, although it was thought that the accommodation would suffice for 50 years.

There are guided tours at 3 p.m. through the richly decorated interior. There are a number of seventeenth- and eighteenth-century bookcases removed from the old library, among them cases made for the books acquired in 1649. Oak cases of 1719 made for the books presented by George I have been placed in the north and south galleries on the first floor. The oldest possession of the Library is a Hebrew papyrus of the Ten Commandments which dates back to the first century.

We can return across the river by Garret Hostel Lane and the elegant new bridge, the gift of Sir Harry Trusted and his two sons who were 'up' at Trinity Hall. Although it is visually pleasing, both cyclists and pedestrians find its excessive steepness formidable. From it, there are extremely beautiful views of the river bordered by lawns and trees, and the bridges of Trinity and Clare. We enter **Trinity Hall,** a college with a long legal tradition, by a fifteenth-century gateway, to find an attractive garden with a terrace beside the river which is a favourite resort of the Hall students. Here, too, is the charming little sixteenth-century Library, surrounded by flowers in summer. Plans of 1745 to replace it were fortunately abandoned. It is built of brick, with a large stepped gable and Gothic windows. The small door on the upper floor was no doubt formerly reached by an external wooden staircase. The ground floor became the Junior Combination Room in 1934, and the Library above retains its late sixteenth-century bookcases and benches.

The Hall was reconstructed in 1743–5 and enlarged in 1892. The Front Court, at the end of the fourteenth century, was the largest enclosed court yet built. The east range was rebuilt by Salvin after it had been destroyed by fire in 1852, and the other sides were ashlar-faced in 1730–45. In the small North Court towards Garret Hostel Lane one can see unfaced masonry of large blocks of clunch; the main court must have looked like this in the fourteenth century. The small Chapel was licensed in 1352, built by 1366, and extended in 1864. Its chief glory is a fine plaster ceiling of 1730, of segmental-barrel form, with painted shields-of-arms and large sunflowers. The building was too small to accommodate everyone when chapel attendance was still compulsory, so first-year men had to attend, second-year men could please themselves, but third-year men had to be exempted. It is in this chapel that a Master is said to have absent-mindedly returned thanks for 'our creation, preservation, and all the rest of the royal family'.

When we leave Trinity Hall, we turn to the right to see the **Old Schools.** When the new buildings designed by Wilkins for King's had been completed, the college sold their old court to the University in 1829, and some of the buildings on the north and south sides were pulled down. C. R. Cockerell's designs for a new University Library envisaged the removal of all of the old buildings to make way for a complete new court, but this scheme was abandoned. In 1864–7 the south range and part of the west range of the old court of King's were reconstructed by G. G. Scott and the windows on the south side towards King's Chapel were modernised in 1935. Of the buildings in Trinity Lane, only the unfinished Gatehouse was retained, and J. L. Pearson completed this and the remainder of the range in 1890. The two lower storeys of the Gatehouse are mainly original, though much restored; the court side is in a more simple style, and it closely resembles the gate at Queens'. Both sides are in a correct Perpendicular style. Facing us as we enter the court is the west range of the Old Schools. The whole West Court of the Old Schools is now occupied by the Registrary and other University offices.

Cockerell's Neo-Classical building of 1836–42 in Senate House Passage was built as an extension of the old University Library and it is now occupied by the Seeley Historical Library and the Squire Law Library. The ground floor, divided by fluted Doric columns, has a groined vault over the central bay, and the reading-room of the much more lofty floor above has a barrel vault with a heavy diagonal coffering, and transverse tunnel vaults over the side bays. Cockerell

32 *King's College: the Gateway and Screen* (*Wilkins, 1824-*
(*overleaf*) *Trinity College.* 33 *The Library* (*Wren, 1677-9*
34 *King Edward's Tower* (*1428-32*), *the Chapel* (*1555-6*
and the Fountain (*1602, rebuilt 171*

successfully combined Roman styles with his own innovations, and had the other three sides of the projected court been built, the whole group would have been one of the most important neo-Classical works of the period.

Few visitors find their way to the East or Cobble Court of the Old Schools, yet here are the oldest buildings erected for the University and not for colleges. The entrance is through the approach to the Seeley Library. The buildings are severely practical and unpretentious, and only the Regent House contains any notable original stonework. The north range, built of rubble, was begun in about 1350 for a Divinity School, and the first floor is the Regent House, nearly 100 feet in length, now the University Combination Room reserved for members of the Regent House, M.A.s on the staff of the University, temporary members elected by the management committee, and their guests. The original low-pitched roof has its old tie-beams with curved braces, traceried spandrels, and plaster-work of about 1600. The large carpet was designed and made by William Morris. The west range was built from about 1430 to 1460 for the teaching of Canon Law, but it was much altered by Essex in 1732. In 1457–70 the south range was built in brick for the schools of Civil Law and Philosophy and as a Library. The upper floor is the Council Room and an antechamber, the Dome Room, with fine wall panelling.

The **Senate House,** designed by James Gibbs, was built in 1722–30, and it is one of his most important works. It is without doubt one of the finest and most dignified of the Classical buildings in Cambridge. The architect had studied in Rome, and the façades have giant fluted Corinthian pilasters supporting a pedimented entablature and a balustraded parapet. The west end was originally of brick because it was planned to join it to a new range on the east front of the Schools. When this scheme was abandoned, it was completed in stone in 1767–8. The Senate House is normally open to the public from 3.30 to 4.30 from Easter Monday until September 30, and on Saturdays and Sundays for the rest of the year, provided that official ceremonies are not taking place. The interior is rectangular, with a pavement of black and white marble, galleries along three sides, and a coffered plaster ceiling by Italian craftsmen, woodwork by the elder Essex, and white marble statues of the Duke of Somerset, by Rysbrack, and of Pitt, by Nollekens.

5 *Trinity College Library, interior (Wren, 1677-99)*

At the west end there is a semi-elliptical recess with a Doric centre-piece. Here, on a dais, are the chairs of the Chancellor and the Vice-Chancellor, and a number of mid-eighteenth-century tables and chairs. The massive cast-iron railings in front of the Senate House are thought to have been placed there in 1730, but were re-erected in 1789–92. In the middle of the lawn is a bronze copy of the Warwick Vase, erected in 1842.

From King's Parade, the Chapel, the east range of the Old Schools, and the Senate House form a most attractive group, and the large tree near the Chapel, encircled in the spring by crocuses, makes an important contribution to this picturesque scene. Old buildings on the east side of the Old Schools were demolished in 1470–4 and replaced in 1754–8 by a Palladian building faced with Portland stone. Burrough made the plans, but the Chancellor, the Duke of Newcastle, commissioned Stephen Wright to design the elevations and supervise the construction. The five middle bays, with an arched loggia on the ground floor and pedimented windows above, are flanked by recessed bays. The windows of the wings and the centre window are in a Venetian style, and above the cornice is a balustraded parapet with stone vases. The East Room on the upper floor of the central block has a plaster ceiling panelled in bays of geometrical patterns with ornamented ribs, and a cornice of garlands of fruits and flowers. At both ends of the room are alcoves with oak panelling and notable doorways.

In Cambridge, the Senate House designed by Gibbs stands near the Screen, Gateway and the Hall range of King's designed by Wilkins, just as in London Gibbs' St. Martin-in-the-Fields adjoins Wilkins' National Gallery. If the spire of St. Martin's is disregarded, the remainder of the building bears a strong resemblance to the Senate House.

Opposite the Senate House is **Great St. Mary's.** The rebuilding of the University Church, which is also a parish church and the largest in Cambridge, began in 1478. The roof of the nave was finished in 1508 and the tower, with interesting views from its summit, 100 years later. It is one of the finest churches in East Anglia of the Late Perpendicular style, with large windows and battlements. An elaborate portal in the Italianesque style was superimposed on the west doorway between 1575 and 1577, but this was removed in 1851. Two small shops stood on either side of this doorway until they were demolished in 1767, and there were many buildings in the churchyard, including, from 1469 until 1788, the parochial almshouses.

The splendid interior has very tall and slender shafts dividing the nave and aisles into five bays. It is fortunate that when the elder James Essex repaired the nave roof in 1726, he built another roof above and tied the old into the new. The aisle galleries were constructed in 1735. In the eighteenth century the University built a huge structure called the Throne, but commonly known as Golgotha, above the rood-loft, for the Vice-Chancellor, Doctors, Professors and University Officers, and a large pulpit stood in the centre of the nave. These incongruous fittings were removed in 1863. Parish record books from 1504 have been preserved, and the bells have been rung by the Ancient Society of Cambridge Youths since 1724. The University Sermon in Great St. Mary's was a weekly event of importance to both the University and the town until towards the end of the Victorian era. For this church, the Rev. Joseph Jowett, a Fellow of Trinity Hall, composed the famous quarter-hour chimes in 1793. Copied in 1859 for Big Ben, and later for clocks throughout the English-speaking world, they are often known, unfairly to Cambridge, as the Westminster Quarters. A curfew was rung from at least 1664 until 1939, when the great tenor bell rang from 9 to 9.15 p.m. and ended with the number of the day of the month. Until 1929 an apprentices' or bedmakers' bell was rung in the mornings from 5.45 to 6, but no doubt neither category rose so early long before the custom ceased.

Before we visit the next college, we should see the beautiful parish church of **St. Edward King and Martyr,** which is of considerable architectural and historical interest. It may be reached by the passage almost opposite the gate of King's. The earliest part, the base of the west tower, was built early in the thirteenth century. The nave, originally without aisles, was rebuilt with aisles in about 1400, and most of this work remains. When Trinity Hall and Clare Hall lost the use of the church of St. John Zachery, demolished when the site for King's was cleared, Henry VI granted the advowson of the church to Trinity Hall. It thus became a Peculiar, outside the jurisdiction of the diocese; small north and south chapels were added on each side of the chancel for the scholars of Clare Hall and Trinity Hall, and they overlap the nave by one bay. The chancel arcades were built at this time.

The chancel has a very open character, with no altar rails or choir stalls, and a barrel roof of the fifteenth century. G. G. Scott redesigned the east window during restorations of 1858–60, and the other windows have since been altered. During the restorations the pulpit of about 1510, with linenfold panelling, from which Latimer and other famous divines had preached, was discarded, but the Provost preserved it in King's Chapel, and it was returned to St. Edward's in 1949. Not far from the pulpit is the Nightwatchman's Chair made in about 1480, which came from a church in Dorset; it provides a link with King Edward, the patron saint, who was murdered at Corfe Castle in 978. The linenfold panelling of the chair is pure Gothic in character.

St. Edward's is notable for the sermons preached there by both parties during the Reformation, and three of the leading exponents of the new doctrines who were associated with the church were burnt— Thomas Bilney at Norwich, Dr. Robert Barnes at Smithfield and Hugh Latimer at Oxford. A tablet on the north wall commemorates the martyrs: 'To the Glory of God and to honour those from this Parish who in the years 1523 to 1525 met near by at the White Horse Inn and there sought out the principles of the English Reformation.

Thomas Bilney   † 1531

Robert Barnes   † 1540

Hugh Latimer   † 1555

who through faith quenched the violence of fire.'

In the nineteenth century, undergraduates flocked to St. Edward's for nearly eight years to hear Harvey Goodwin preach, and here, too, F. D. Maurice exerted an enormous influence at a time when many pulpits were closed to him.

From St. Edward's, we continue along the Passage to Peas Hill, where a restrained new hostel for King's has been erected at the corner. The Guildhall, a dignified, well-proportioned brick edifice mainly built in 1938–9, and a modern block for **Caius,** are on opposite sides of the Market Square. The college building, designed by Murray Easton, 1934, is definitely of the twentieth century. With the exception of a recessed bay at the corner of Rose Crescent, and the side towards the court, which is quite unlike the Market Square frontage, it is of white Portland stone. The bookshop opposite the Senate House is the oldest in Great Britain; books have been sold here continuously to successive generations of students since 1581. It was here that Alexander and Daniel Macmillan, the grandfather of Harold Macmillan, laid the foundations of the great publishing firm.

The Caius building erected by Waterhouse in 1870 was much admired when it was new, but few would defend it today. Ponderous and assertive, it dominates the Senate House and has no regard for the older buildings near by. The tall and heavy tower has large chimneys, a spire, statues in niches, and intricately but mechanically carved stonework. We enter the college through the Gate of Honour in Senate House Passage, completed in 1575 after the death of Caius, but to his designs. It is one of the most frequently photographed of Cambridge monuments, and of a novel design, probably inspired by a Roman tomb. The Gate has three storeys, with Ionic pilasters on the ground storey, and rich decoration. The stone was originally painted white, with some parts coloured and gilded, and sundials on each face of the hexagonal tower have been recently restored.

Dr. Caius designed three gates to symbolise stages in a student's college life. He would enter through the small Gate of Humility, now in the Master's Garden, and often pass through the Gate of Virtue during his years of residence. He would finally walk through the Gate of Honour to receive his degree. The beautiful Gate of Virtue is an architectural landmark, since it is one of a few constructions of its time in a pure Renaissance style. To the east and west are stone ranges erected by Dr. Caius in 1565–7, on the south side is the Chapel, and the fourth side was left open apart from the wall, because he considered that it would be more healthy. The Chapel was built of clunch and brick in about 1393, but was lengthened in 1637, and the interior remodelled. Considerable alterations were made in 1716–26, when the walls were ashlared and the massive buttresses added. Within it, one immediately notices the ceiling decorated with gilt suns, and the striking monument to Dr. Caius, raised to its present position on the wall in 1637, although it was at ground level when it was placed in the Chapel in 1575. Another monument commemorates Dr. Perse, who died in 1615, leaving money to found a 'grammar free school' on land near Corpus, where it remained until moved to Hills Road in 1890.

The small Gonville Court beyond the Chapel was the first to be built, and 140 years elapsed before it was complete. Burrough refaced it in ashlar in 1753. To the left is the entrance to the Hall and Library, both on the first floor, built by Salvin in 1853. Alterations are in progress, and in 1963 only the outer walls are still standing. William Harvey, the father of English medicine, Jeremy Taylor, the distinguished theologian, and Sir Thomas Gresham, the financier who designed and built the Royal Exchange, were students of the college. We return to Trinity Street through Tree Court, where Waterhouse's building is reminiscent of some of the châteaux of the Loire, though more restrained than the street frontage. Caius spread across the road to St. Michael's Court in 1903.

The church of **St. Michael**, although damaged by fire in 1849 and restored by Sir George Gilbert Scott, has not been much altered since Hervey de Stanton, Chancellor of the Exchequer to Edward II, rebuilt it after he had founded Michaelhouse in 1323. He died in 1327 before it was complete, and is buried in the chancel. Other early colleges shared churches with parishioners, but St. Michael's is unique because it was appropriated to the college. The chancel is large by comparison with the nave, since here the scholars of Michaelhouse, who were all M.A.s and priests, performed their religious observances, while the nave served for preaching and disputations. The choir stalls are fifteenth century and there is a full-length portrait of Charles I given to the church in about 1660. East of the south aisle is a small chapel, presumably the founder's. The church is at present rarely used.

We continue along Trinity Street, passing a notable late eighteenth-century building in red brick at the corner of Green Street, and the Turk's Head Grill, once the Turk's Head Coffee House, built in about 1600; it is one of the only two elaborate domestic buildings of about the same date still standing in the town. **Trinity** Great Gate, almost the only remaining part of King's Hall, was built in 1528–35, though the lower portion may have been constructed in about 1490. It has a large entrance for vehicles and a small door for pedestrians. The massive oak main gate was hung in 1523. The seven coloured shields commemorate Edward III and his six sons; the third from the left bears the arms of Edward the Black Prince, and the fourth, those of the King himself. The blank shield is that of William of Hatfield, who died in infancy. Below are two shields charged with ostrich feathers. The statue of Henry VIII, in an elaborately carved niche, was put up in 1615, and the sceptre is actually a wooden chair-leg. On the court side of the Gate there is a single broad archway, with a statue of James I in the central niche, flanked by his Queen, Anne of Denmark, and Prince Charles. Although these statues were carved in London, the stone came from the Cambridgeshire villages of Barrington and Eversden. In the eighteenth century there was an observatory on top of the Gate.

Trinity Great Court is the largest of any college in Cambridge or Oxford. Most of the buildings are not particularly impressive, but the size of the court and the admirable Fountain makes it the best known in Cambridge. We should first turn to the right. Thackeray occupied the ground-floor rooms adjoining the Gate, Macaulay those next to the Chapel, and Sir Isaac Newton those above. The large Chapel, almost wholly in the Gothic style, was erected in 1555–67. Some of the stone used, nearly 3,000 loads in the first year, came from the Franciscan Friary, and some from Ramsey Abbey. In the antechapel is a statue of Newton, a masterpiece by Roubiliac (1755), and seated figures of Bacon, Barrow, Macaulay, Whewell and Tennyson, all of the nineteenth century except the latter. The magnificent screen with Corinthian columns which separates the antechapel from the chapel was erected during the mastership of Bentley (1700–42), and the stalls, panelling and the baldacchino belong to the same period. The decoration of the flat roof, the wall paintings and stained glass, was executed in 1867–75.

King Edward's Tower, erected in 1428–32, is the oldest building in the court and the first gateway-tower with four turrets to be built in Cambridge. It originally stood near the sundial, but was taken down and re-erected when Nevile demolished old buildings between 1597 and 1605 to create a regular court. Regular, but not symmetrical; no side is as long as the side opposite, none of the angles is a right angle, the Gatehouses are not in the centre of the ranges, and the Fountain is not in the middle of the court. The niche and statue of Edward III were put up in 1601. The picturesque timber bell-turret is modern, but it is a copy of the original.

The large and magnificent Master's Lodge in the north-west corner reflects the mode of life of eighteenth-century Heads of Colleges. The big drawing-room has a fine plaster ceiling and a decorated fireplace, with state bedrooms above. There is another early fireplace in the dining-room. Bentley put in the beautiful main staircase in 1710. The Hall, built by Nevile in 1604–8, is the largest in Cambridge and a copy of the hall of the Middle Temple, to which it corresponds in length, breadth and height. Some of the stone for it came from the Castle. There are large bay windows containing a great deal of heraldic glass on both sides of the dais, and a hammerbeam roof, one of the most remarkable timber roofs of its time. The hexagonal timber lantern, in three stages, is a most graceful structure, and the screen is richly carved. The Stuart Royal Arms surmount the panelling on the north wall, and the portraits include Bacon, Dryden, Melbourne, Tennyson, Lord Baldwin and Sir J. J. Thomson. The Hall was formerly heated by an iron brazier purchased in 1702–3; it was removed in 1866. The Kitchen was built at the same time as the Hall, and it was equivalent to three storeys in height, and open to the hammerbeam roof; it is now (1964) being modernised.

The water for the beautiful late Elizabethan octagonal Fountain, the only large ornamental fountain of the period still in existence in England, comes from a field over 1,800 yards distant, through an underground conduit originally constructed by the Franciscans in 1325. Nevile built the Queen's Gate in the south range, and the statue of Queen Elizabeth was put up when it was completed in 1597. On the far side of the Screens we emerge on to a Tribune built in 1682 to render this side of the court more in keeping with the remainder. Nevile's Court was finished in an Italianate style in 1612 at the sole expense of the Master. Originally, it was only three-fifths of its present length, and was closed by a wall with a large central gate, re-erected later as the entrance to Bishop's Hostel in Trinity Lane. The cloisters, with their stone columns, are original, but the fronts of the north and south ranges were rebuilt by Essex in 1755. He altered the attics into a full storey and added the balustraded parapet. The south range was, in fact, almost entirely rebuilt. The rooms of Lord Byron were in this court.

Sir Christopher Wren's Library was begun in 1676, the architect making no charge for his services, and in 1676–81 the north and south ranges of the court were extended to join it. Wren first suggested a circular domed building, but the plan adopted resembles Sansovino's Library of St. Mark at Venice. The simple, 150-feet-long rectangular building is one of Wren's masterpieces. It is raised on columns, with a cloister below, and the floor of the Library is at the same level as the adjoining first-floor rooms. The west side towards the river has three large doorways and small windows on the ground floor, but the large Library windows are identical on both sides. The statues on the roof represent Divinity, Law, Physics and Mathematics. Professor Pryme, who was a student at Trinity 1799–1803, relates in his autobiography that, 20 years earlier, practical jokers bribed the college barber to let them have the Dons' wigs, and placed them on the heads of the statues. On Sunday, the Dons were much perturbed to find their best wigs missing, but saw them adorning the figures on the Library when they came out of Hall.

A staircase on the north side of the court leads to the interior, open to visitors on weekdays, 1.0–4.0 p.m. It is more spacious than one would imagine from the exterior. Bookcases run along the walls and also at right angles to them, to form 30 cubicles. Wren said that this arrangement 'must needes prove very convenient and gracefull, and the best way for the students will be to have a little square table in each Celle with two Chaires'. On the Norway oak bookcases, made by a local carpenter, Grinling Gibbons carved exquisite arabesques and wreaths of fruit and flowers in limewood. Marble busts, many by Roubiliac, are placed against the ends of the bookcases, and at the far end of the room is Thorwaldsen's statue of Byron. It was intended for Westminster Abbey, but was not accepted, and remained in the Custom House for about 12 years before it was given to Trinity. The south stained glass window, designed by Cipriani and put up in 1774, depicts Fame introducing Bacon and Newton to George III. Some of the treasures of the Library are displayed in table-cases, among them illuminated manuscripts, a book in which Milton wrote *Comus*, *Lycidas* and other poems, the first draft of *Paradise Lost*, and manuscripts of Thackeray, Tennyson and others.

A narrow passage in the south-west corner of Great Court leads to Bishop's Hostel, a modest brick building with a domestic rather than a collegiate appearance, erected shortly before the Library, and the entrance to New Court, designed by Wilkins in a Tudor-Gothic style and constructed in 1823–5. From the gateway on the far side an avenue leads over a bridge and through splendid iron gates to the Backs. The three-arched Bridge, a Classical architectural work, and plain by comparison with those on either side at Clare and St. John's, but blending well with the Library, was rebuilt by Essex in 1763–5.

St. John's may be reached by a small iron bridge over a stream dividing the grounds of the two colleges, but to see the oldest part first it is better to return to the street. If we do so through New Court and Trinity Lane, it is possible to see the unfaced ancient walls of the south side of Great Court, with striking tall chimneys. We turn to the left into St. John's Street. The little garden across the road was the site of the church of All Saints-in-the-Jewry, demolished in 1865. Until then, the outer wall of the church tower reached to the edge of the pavement, and pedestrians walked through a passage beneath the tower.

St. John's possesses the most handsome of the gateway-towers. The striking ornamentation commemorates the founder, the Lady Margaret Beaufort, and the daisies or marguerites are an allusion to her name. The curious animals with goats' heads, antelopes' bodies and elephants' tails are called yales. On one side there is a portcullis, and on the other a rose, both surmounted by crowns. The statue of St. John in a niche above was placed there in 1662. All of these decorations were skilfully recoloured some years ago. The two turrets towards the street had to be rebuilt on a steel frame in 1934–5, when cracks caused by traffic vibration appeared. The buildings on either side are of two storeys, with irregular windows, and the upper room to the left was formerly the Library.

First Court, built in brick in 1511–20, is now incomplete; the north range containing the old Chapel was demolished, and the south range was altered and ashlar-faced by Essex in 1772–5. Stone kerbs in the grass indicate the position of the old Chapel. The West range has the entrance to the Screens passage in the centre, the Kitchens to the left and the Hall to the right. The Master's Lodge, originally to the right of the Hall, was placed elsewhere when the Hall was lengthened by 40 feet, and a second oriel window added, in 1862–5.

The Chapel was designed by Sir G. G. Scott and built in 1864–9. The architect proposed to restore and enlarge the old Chapel, but the Fellows decided to demolish and rebuild. He designed a grandiose

St. John's College. 36 The 'Bridge of Sighs' (Hutchinson, 183
37 The Combination Room (1600

isolated building unrelated to the rest of the college, mainly in a thirteenth-century style, with a tower 163 feet high, and an apse reminiscent of the Sainte-Chapelle in Paris. The antechapel is a transept at the west end, with a crossing tower between it and the Chapel. Arches in the antechapel once gave access to a chantry erected by Bishop Fisher in the old Chapel; as he was executed, he was not buried in it.

The monument of Hugh Ashton, who died in 1522, was removed to its present position from a chantry in the old Chapel. It has a recumbent effigy of him, and in accordance with his will, a second effigy of a corpse lies below. Ashton's rebus, an ash leaf growing out of a tun, is carved in the stone canopy above the tomb and also incorporated in the iron grating. The late thirteenth-century piscina to the right of the altar, and 32 stalls on each side, were removed from the older building. The range facing the antechapel was built in 1855, and it was extended to the north by buildings designed by Sir Edward Maufe, with a façade in Bridge Street, mainly put up in 1938–9 and finally completed in 1942. Many old shops and houses which had occupied the site were demolished, and the road widened.

We return to First Court, where above the doorway to the Screens is a statue of the Lady Margaret. The Hall has its original hammerbeam roof, and windows separated by buttresses. Up to the first oriel window the Hall is original; the second oriel window was added when the building was enlarged, and the panelling behind the High Table was then set back. A portrait of the foundress hangs above the High Table, and other portraits include Bishop Fuller and William Wordsworth. In *The Prelude* the poet describes his college rooms:

> *Right underneath the college kitchens made*
> *A humming sound, less tuneable than bees,*
> *But hardly less industrious.*

His rooms were added to the Kitchen in 1893, but an upper window has a memorial inscription.

Second Court was built in 1598–1602, and a rainwater-head dated 1599 can be seen between the second and third windows of the north side. The designer's drawings, the earliest of any Cambridge college still to survive, are in the Library. The court was built with money given by the Countess of Shrewsbury, and her statue is above the Gatehouse. The Master's Gallery, almost 50 yards long, once occupied the whole of the first floor on the north side. In old records, such galleries are often called 'ambulatorium magistri', so they were probably intended to be places where the Master could take exercise in bad weather. About 45 feet at the west end was partitioned off to make a space for a staircase to the Library, and in 1863–5 the main part was converted into a Combination Room. It is now 93 feet long, and one of the finest rooms of its type in England, with a rich plaster ceiling made in 1600–1 and panelling of about the same time.

The Library, entered from Third Court, was built in 1623–4, and the initials I.L.C.S. (*Johannes Lincolniensis, Custos Sigilli*) on the gable overlooking the river commemorate John Williams, then Bishop of Lincoln and Lord Keeper of the Privy Seal, who contributed two-thirds of the cost. He was a former Sizar and Fellow, and eventually became Archbishop of York. The Library, 100 feet long, is of special architectural interest because the tall two-light windows are a very early example of the Gothic Revival. The beautiful original bookcases are not detached from the side-walls as in earlier libraries.

The south and west ranges of the court were built in 1669–73, and the date 1671 appears on the west gable towards the river. The south range is two rooms in thickness; it is the first college building with this feature throughout. Through a gateway we come to the famous 'Bridge of Sighs', built in 1831 to the designs of Henry Hutchinson. This picturesque bridge is a very successful accomplishment both externally and internally. The tall and narrow interior commands beautiful views of the river in both directions, seen through its unglazed Gothic windows. On one side is the bridge built by Robert Grumbold in 1709–12 to designs based on suggestions made by Wren, a notable structure with a balustraded parapet and panels adorned with carvings of a Roman type. At the end are two piers surmounted by heraldic beasts. Both Grumbold and Wren recommended that it should be placed to prolong the axis of the three courts, but the college authorities wished it to be at the end of the kitchen lane.

When New Court was constructed in 1825–31, it was the largest single building of any college. In a Neo-Gothic style, it has a symmetrical façade with a recessed centre, and a screen wall with unglazed windows connecting the two projecting side ranges resembles Wilkins' screen at King's. Behind a vaulted cloister with a central gateway rises the high middle section of the main building, with four turrets and a glazed lantern with pinnacles, irreverently called the 'Wedding Cake'. When New Court is seen rising beyond the landscaped grounds, its unusual silhouette is pleasingly romantic. The cost was £78,000, of which £65,000 had to be borrowed, and the debt was not cleared until 1857, when interest charges had amounted to £41,000.

St. John's Wilderness, near Queens' Road, is at its best in the Spring, when thousands of daffodils, primroses and other flowers are in bloom beneath the trees. In 1952, Dr. Thomas Sharp planned alterations to the landscaped grounds, and a formal garden was laid out to the north of the walk leading to the Backs. We leave by the back gate. The college playing-fields across the road are on the site of an Anglo-Saxon cemetery from which hundreds of skeletons were removed. We turn to the right and soon come to Westminster College, built in 1899 by Hare. It is not part of the University, but a Presbyterian training college. In Northampton Street it is possible to glimpse the gabled seventeenth-century Merton Hall and the **School of Pythagoras**, the oldest secular building in the city, best seen from the yard of the Merton Arms. It has a vaulted ground floor and a large hall with a big fireplace on the first floor.

On the left, the spire of St. Peter's rises above old cottages skilfully transformed into an attractive house, and some very successful modern flats for old people. The ancient White Horse Inn at the corner is now the Folk Museum, and a few yards beyond is St. Peter's church, the smallest in Cambridge, with a Norman doorway and font. At the top of the hill is the Shire Hall and the Castle Mound; a fine view is obtained from the summit. As we descend again to the crossroads, St. Giles is a modern church but preserves a fine early Norman chancel arch from a former St. Giles. A short distance down Chesterton Lane brings us to the hostel designed for Clare by Mr. D. W. Roberts in an attractive contemporary style. Bedsitting-rooms on four floors, each with a small triangular dressing-room, have a saw-tooth façade, so that every room faces to the south.

We return to the crossroads and turn left. The red brick range of **Magdalene** facing the street does not look ancient, since it was restored in 1875, yet the whole court was built of brick-faced clunch from about 1430 to 1580, and the Renaissance entrance gateway in 1585. The buildings in this court were refaced with stucco in 1759–60, but this has lately been removed to reveal the beautiful rose-coloured bricks. On the north side is the Library and Chapel, and on the east of the Hall, surmounted by an attractive lantern, the Buttery with a Combination Room above. The four monasteries which supported the original college probably each built some chambers to their own design; this would account for the variations in the doorways and windows. Dr. Caius, who was a student in 1529–31, described 'different monasteries building different portions; thus Ely one chamber, Walden a second and Ramsey a third'. The arms of the monasteries above the doorways are not original.

Staircase 'E' of the south range preserves the original arrangements for students' chambers. The room to the west on the upper floor has exposed clunch walls, with partitions forming three small study cubicles, and a garderobe and lavatory recess in the wall. This unique survival is not open to the public. The Chapel, though restored and lengthened, is in part the original chapel of Buckingham College, and in particular the roof. South-west of the Chapel, the drawing-room and dining-room of the Master's Lodge were converted into a Library in 1835. There are two Elizabethan or Jacobean fireplaces, and a notable altar-relief made in 1756 and representing in plaster the Three Marys and an angel beside the Sepulchre after the Resurrection; this was removed from the Chapel during the restoration of 1847–51.

The small Hall of 1519 has also been much altered, but the windows are original. Above the High Table, and occupying the whole of the wall above the panelling, are the arms of Queen Anne, with two smaller achievements on each side. At the south end a beautiful double staircase built in 1714 leads to the Gallery and Combination Room. Between the staircases, the screen and gallery-front contain pieces of late sixteenth- or early seventeenth-century carving. Among the portraits are Charles Kingsley, Samuel Pepys as a young man by Sir Peter Lely, and Dr. A. C. Benson. In the Second Court is the fine Pepys Building. The diarist gave money towards its construction and bequeathed his library to the college. The inscription Bibliotheca Pepysiana, 1724, with his arms in the pediment of the central window and his motto, was put up when his books arrived. The front is quite unlike the remainder of the building. Pepys' library of 3,000 volumes, kept in the original cases of red oak, is now in the south wing. The cases have glass doors, and the smaller books stand on little pedestals shaped like the back of a book, so that the tops of all the books are on the same level. A college register contains the following entry relating to Samuel Pepys, Scholar: 'Oct. 21st., 1653. Mem. That Pepys and Hind were solomnely admonished by myself and Mr. Hill for having been scandalously in drink the night before. This was done in the presence of all the ffellows then resident in Mr. Hill's chamber. Joh. Wood, Reg.'. The manuscripts of the diaries are also in the Library.

The Master's Lodge was built in 1835, and a brick range beside the river in 1908–9. More recent additions to Magdalene lie behind the timber-framed houses, some now adapted for college use, on the opposite side of the street. Brick houses were similarly adapted in 1925 to form the attractive Mallory Court, named after the Magdalene man who died on Mount Everest. Sir Edwin Lutyens' red brick range of 1931–2 in Benson Court was planned to have two other ranges, and Mallory Court and the houses in Magdalene Street, the best surviving mediaeval domestic buildings in the city, would have been demolished to make way for them. There has, however, lately been a greater recognition of the need to preserve the few remaining good examples of non-collegiate building, and the picturesque group is now carefully maintained. An entrance beside the post office, formerly the Cross Keys Inn, leads to houses built in 1952–6 in a style reminiscent of the South Bank Exhibition. Other buildings, in pleasing contemporary styles, have recently been put up near the river.

Beyond the Great Bridge is the small church of **St. Clement**, with a nave of the late twelfth or early thirteenth century. The tower was erected in 1821 with a legacy from the Rev. William Cole, a famous local eighteenth-century man who filled nearly 100 folio volumes, now in the British Museum, with notes about the antiquities of the county. On the side of the tower facing Bridge Street is the ingenious inscription 'Deum Cole', meaning 'Worship God', which also commemorates the name of the man who provided the funds to rebuild the tower. It formerly had a spire which has been taken down. Behind the church stands the Old Vicarage, a timber-framed house of about 1600. Nos. 15

and 16 Bridge Street, on the corner of Jordan's Yard, are typical late mediaeval town houses with plastered timber-framed walls, roofs of tiles, and projecting first and second floors. They were built early in the sixteenth century, and Nos. 1–4a in Jordan's Yard at the same time. These houses have been altered, and at present have a derelict appearance.

Multitudes of people visit and photograph the Norman church of the **Holy Sepulchre** because it is one of only five round churches surviving in the country. As a rule, round churches were built by Orders founded to guard the Holy Land and the Holy Sepulchre, but there is no proof that the Cambridge church originated in this way. It is known that between 1114 and 1130, members of the fraternity of the Holy Sepulchre were granted the site for their church, and that the circular nave and ambulatory and a small chancel were built during the first half of the twelfth century; a north chapel was added later. In the fifteenth century a polygonal belfry was placed above the nave, most of the windows were altered, and the chancel arch and north chapel were rebuilt.

In 1841 the Cambridge Camden Society thoroughly restored the church, but the twelfth-century style was carefully retained or re-created. The fifteenth-century belfry was demolished, and a stone vault erected over the circular nave. The vault over the aisle and the west doorway were rebuilt, the clerestory windows altered to conform to one of the twelfth century that had survived, and windows of the same style replaced Gothic windows in the aisle. The east and north walls of the chancel and the north chancel were rebuilt and a bell-turret added. The south aisle of the chancel dates from this restoration. The erection of a stone altar and credence-table caused a lawsuit, and the church was closed from 1843 to 1845, until they were declared to be illegal and were removed.

To reach **Jesus** College, we take the next road to the left and soon come to the four-column Ionic portico of the Pitt Club. In spite of its late eighteenth-century appearance, the building was not erected until 1863, when it was opened as a swimming-bath by the Roman Bath Co. Ltd. It later became the home of the Pitt Club, which is no longer political; its 200 members claim that it is the most comfortable and civilised club in Cambridge. 'Little Trinity', a three-storey early eighteenth-century building, is probably the finest private house in the city. At the corner of Park Street a mediaeval stone bridge which once spanned the King's Ditch was discovered about a yard below the surface of the road.

I should imagine that less than one in a hundred of the people who visit the colleges near the Backs go to see Jesus, yet the Chapel is of very great interest and beauty, and there are other survivals from the Nunnery of St. Radegund. We enter by a gate in Jesus Lane built in 1703 by Robert Grumbold, and walk along the 'chimney', a path between two walls, to the Gatehouse built by Bishop Alcock soon after he began to adapt the conventual buildings in 1497. Here, as in numerous other places in the college, is the founder's rebus, a cock standing on a globe.

The ranges on either side were built a little later, and that to the left of the gate was at first a grammar school. The buildings were originally of two storeys, and the addition of a third storey in 1718 has rendered the Gatehouse less impressive. To the right is the Master's Lodge; the nave of the nuns' church extended as far as the porch of the Lodge. Beyond the gate, the range facing us was put up in 1638–40. To the right is Cloister Court, where all of the buildings are of monastic origin, although there have been alterations since Alcock's time. He increased the height to three storeys and inserted the fine timber ceilings in the cloisters. The open arches of yellow brick were constructed by Essex.

As the Bishop's college was intended to have a Master, six Fellows and only a few scholars, the nuns' church was much too large. The nave and chancel aisles were destroyed, and a wall built to cut off the western part of the nave. This portion was converted into chambers, and later became the Master's Lodge. In the east wall a large Perpendicular window replaced five lancets, and the cloister was enlarged to the south by including the aisle of the church. All of the Chapter House of about 1230 was demolished, with the exception of the west wall, in which the doorway and windows were blocked up. The beautiful early work now to be seen remained concealed until 1893, when one of the Honorary Fellows, who had noticed indications of their existence during repairs about 50 years earlier, obtained permission to remove some of the plaster from the wall.

The present beautiful Chapel consists of the antechapel, formerly the eastern part of the conventual church nave, the transepts and the choir. On the west wall is a striking white marble monument to Tobias Rustat, Yeoman of the Robes to Charles II, who died in 1695. Two cherubs draw aside draperies to reveal a portrait in a medallion, and the inscription-cartouche below is bordered by garlands of fruit and flowers. Carving of about 1500 has been incorporated into benches. The forward extensions are surmounted by the Bishop's rebus, and the poppy-heads have seated figures of a bishop and of doctors of divinity.

The nave was built in about 1200, and original aisle piers can be seen in the west wall. The north transept, with three Norman windows now blocked, is the oldest part, and was probably built in about 1160. The tracery in the east wall was put in by Pugin when he restored the Chapel in 1849–53. To the north and south of the chancel are exquisite lancets with slender shafts and moulded capitals. Pugin reconstructed the east end of the magnificent thirteenth-century chancel, putting in five lancet windows based on surviving fragments of the original work; the screen and stalls, the altar, and the tiles in the crossing and the choir. He designed the stained glass and the lectern copied from that at St. Mark's in Venice. A thirteenth-century double piscina has interesting round arches to form two pointed ones, and a frame with dog-tooth decoration. Further repairs were carried out in 1864–7, when Bodley strengthened and refaced the tower, and had new ceilings designed by Morris put into the nave, crossing tower and chancel. A little later, most of the windows were reglazed by Morris Faulkner & Co., almost all of them designed by Burne-Jones.

The conventual kitchens were on the ground floor of the north range, with the refectory, now the Hall, above. Bishop Alcock heightened the walls and refaced them with brick, and inserted new windows and a new roof. The Hall has a very beautiful three-sided oriel window, the transoms carved with foliage, and the opening into the oriel is a lofty arch with fine carving on the soffit. The armorial stained glass is by Morris. A small oriel window projects from the west wall, and the other windows have had their sills lowered. The panelling of the screen and the dais, where there is a large achievement of the Stuart Royal Arms, was executed in 1703. In 1875 the Hall was lengthened by Waterhouse, and the staircase on the north side was added. Alcock's rebus occurs in many places, and the bronze cock was presented to the college in 1897. Among the portraits are the Founder; Henry VIII; Cranmer, who was a Fellow; Laurence Sterne; and Tobias Rustat, painted by Sir Peter Lely.

Laurence Sterne, who entered Jesus as a poor sizar, was the great-grandson of a former Master, Richard Sterne, who was imprisoned in the Tower during the Civil War by Cromwell, but regained the Mastership at the Restoration and later became Archbishop of York. Another famous Jesus man was Samuel Taylor Coleridge. The Old Library has bookcases of 1663–79 standing at right angles to the walls between the windows, and the roof of about 1500 is divided by massive intersecting moulded timbers. Small Doric columns above the ends of the book-cases give additional support to it. The Bishop's cocks occur again in the east window, where much of the glass is original.

Jesus College is fortunate in having a very large site, and the nine-teenth- and twentieth-century buildings have been placed round spacious lawns. In 1822 the east range of Cloister Court was continued in white brick, the window shapes conforming to the old work, and when Waterhouse built a detached range north of Outer Court in 1869–70, he too retained two-light windows. In this range he placed an asymmetrical tower. Another detached range in bright red brick, with a central gatehouse, was built in 1884–5. Waterhouse's building and the 1822 range were connected in 1922–3 by Morley Horder, and in 1931 the same architect built the ranges on three sides of Chapel Court, one adorned by a coat of arms and two angels by Eric Gill. The brick chosen blends admirably with the stone of the Chapel.

To reach the next college, **Sidney Sussex**, we return down Jesus Lane and turn left. The entrance lodge was built by Wyatville, who also faced the buildings of both courts with cement, and introduced the gables and battlements, to give the present Tudor-Gothic appearance. His alterations created a unified E-plan design out of two dissimilar courts. Hall Court, to the left of the gateway, is structurally the building put up by Ralph Symons in 1595–98. There are three ranges, with a wall on the fourth side. The Hall, in the north half of the east range, has panelled walls and a plaster ceiling with stucco ornament. At the High Table end is an original large semi-circular bay window, with a symmetrical bay on the Kitchen and Lodge side. There is a portrait of the Foundress, but the most famous is of Oliver Cromwell, who entered the college as a Fellow-Commoner in 1616. In 1766 the Master was informed in an anonymous letter that the writer wished to present to the college a portrait in crayons of Oliver Cromwell, and the identity of the donor was not known until 1780.

The range with an arcaded walk north-east of Hall Court was built in 1890, and the beautiful gardens were first laid out in the eighteenth century. The notable old gateway of 1762 has been rebuilt in the wall towards Jesus Lane. In the Second Court is the Chapel designed by Essex in 1776–82 to replace an earlier building of 1600. It was rebuilt and lengthened by T. H. Lyon in 1912, with a barrel-vaulted plaster ceiling and elaborate oak panelling on the walls. The large painting above the altar is by G. B. Pittoni, an early example of Italian rococo, bought in 1783 for 20 guineas. To the right of the sanctuary is a small Lady Chapel. The Library, between the Chapel and the Master's Lodge, retains the fitting of 1778, and contains a fifteenth-century chest with elaborate ironwork. Sir Francis Clarke's range of 1628, forming the east side of Chapel Court, remains, though much altered. Beyond this are twentieth-century buildings, an L-shaped brick building of 1923, and a range facing Sussex Street designed by E. R. Barrow and erected in 1938–9. On the college side, access to the rooms is on a terrace, and there are shops on the ground floor of the street side.

Beyond Sidney is **Holy Trinity** church, at the corner of Market Street, formerly Shoemaker Row, and until the end of the eighteenth century so narrow that only a few feet separated the overhanging upper storeys of the houses. Holy Trinity is famous for its connection with the Evangelical Movement. The first church on the site is believed to have been destroyed by a fire of 1174 which caused much damage in a large part of the town. The rebuilt church was extensively altered in the late fourteenth century, when arcades north and south of the nave, the north and south aisles and the west tower were built. The large transepts, a striking feature of the church, and the clerestory of the nave, were rebuilt in the fifteenth century. Buttresses had to be placed against the north-east and south-east piers of the tower because the widening of the nave had removed the support given by the earlier arcades. The south aisle was widened in the sixteenth century, and galleries were erected later when the Trinity Lectureship attracted large congregations. These have now been removed, but there is still an early nineteenth-century gallery in the south transept, constructed during the incumbency of the very popular Rev. Charles Simeon, who was vicar of the parish for 54 years. A large wall monument in the chancel commemorates him. The chancel was rebuilt in 1834, the transept arches in about 1851, and the spire in 1901.

We come next to **Christ's** College. The early buildings had walls of clunch and brick which by the end of the seventeenth century looked so worn and ugly that repairs had to be made. The street frontage was ashlar-faced early in the eighteenth century, and extended in 1895–7, when Bodley lengthened the Library. The Gateway of 1505–11 closely resembles that of St. John's, the Lady Margaret's other foundation, and has a large carved and coloured coat-of-arms above the arch. The figure of the foundress is modern, but the doorway with linenfold panelling is original.

Most of the First Court was complete when the Lady Margaret died in 1509, and although Essex ashlared the buildings and altered windows and doorways in 1758–69, the modest scale was preserved. The Hall was altered in 1723, and in 1875 G. G. Scott rebuilt it with old materials, raised the walls 6 feet and built a new oriel. Additional dining accommodation was gained in 1928 when arches were made at the back of the gallery to provide access to the former Combination Room. There are portraits of the foundress, Charles Darwin, John Milton and William Paley. The Lady Margaret occupied the first floor and attics of the Master's Lodge, and heraldic carving at the bottom of the oriel of her chamber is original; the design is almost identical with that on the former Lodge at St. John's. An adjacent room has two small windows looking into the Hall.

The picturesque top of the Chapel turret rises above the north range. The antechapel is a low room with a chamber above, the floor supported by four wooden columns put up in 1661. The timber roof of the Chapel is original, and the notable panelling was made by John Austin in 1701–2. The north windows have stained glass of the late fifteenth and early sixteenth century, and the large brass eagle lectern, probably from God's House, is one of the finest Pre-Reformation examples in England, and resembles a lectern in St. Mark's, Venice. Near the organ is a striking black and white marble monument to Sir

Thomas Baines and Sir John Finch, completed by Joseph Catterns in 1684. Two pedestals support oval portrait medallions, flanked by flower garlands, and two cherubs are perched on the corners of the pedestal-cappings.

In the Second Court there is an uninteresting range of chambers built in 1823, but facing us is Fellows' Building, erected in 1640–3, one of the most interesting buildings of its period in England, a large symmetrical detached block of three storeys with attics, placed some distance away from the First Court. The unknown designer introduced two features not hitherto seen in Cambridge—upright windows with a mullion and transom cross, and attic windows, some with triangular and others with segmental pediments, behind balusters set diagonally, as on Clare Bridge. At each end of the block are large Ionic columns, and there are three doorways, the larger central one with a triangular pediment and the others with segmental pediments.

In 1889 another range of similar design was put up to the north-east of the earlier building, and in 1948 and 1952 two ranges designed by Professor Richardson were built to form a third court. These ranges have a twentieth-century lack of ornamentation and the stone facing is handsome. A rectangular bathing-pool and a small eighteenth-century summer-house are in a far corner of the beautiful garden. Beside the pool are three stone busts, one of John Milton, and a draped urn, on tapering pedestals. Milton was a Pensioner from 1625 to 1632, and his rooms were on the left side of First Court as it is entered from the street, on the first floor of the first staircase. He was not popular with his fellows, as he was held to be 'not ignorant of his own parts'. In the garden is the celebrated mulberry tree said to have been planted by him. J. W. Clark suggested that the tree was probably one of 300 planted in the year of Milton's birth, but a former Master thus dealt with that heresy: 'The suggestion that the object of wider interest than anything else in Christ's—"Milton's mulberry tree"—is probably the last of that purchase, is the one crime among a thousand virtues of the present Registry of the University'.

Charles Darwin entered Christ's two centuries later, and two famous metaphysicians of the seventeenth century, Ralph Cudworth and Henry More, were contemporaries at the college. William Paley entered in 1759 and remained until 1776, apart from an absence of a year.

Christopher Tancred, who endowed four scholarships in divinity, had five sisters but no son. He explained his gift by saying that 'he could not bear that an estate so commodious by the improvements and industry of himself and ancestors should be dismembered by a distribution among heirs female'. Christ's has for long welcomed non-European students.

Between Christ's and Emmanuel is the most important commercial redevelopment yet completed in the city centre—Bradwell's Court, a pedestrian shopping precinct, and the large and pleasing Prudential block of shops and offices. A recent addition to **Emmanuel** College on the opposite corner is much less successful—in fact the new kitchens and dining hall are extremely ugly externally. Emmanuel is of special interest to American visitors, since so many of its seventeenth-century Puritan scholars sought freedom across the Atlantic, including John Harvard, who entered as a Pensioner in 1627.

The main front of the college was rebuilt by Essex and completed in 1775, with cloisters towards the court. We should go first to the small New Court to the north of the Hall range, as in spite of its name, this was originally the first court of the college; it was entered from Emmanuel Street. If we ignore the dull nineteenth-century building towards the street, the remainder has not been greatly changed since the founder adopted what remained of the Dominican Priory. To demonstrate his Puritan sympathies, he converted the Friars' church into a hall, and the frater into a chapel, orientated to the north. In the remarkable hall range, three original buttresses survive. The founder's chapel on the east side later became a library, but in 1932–3 it was converted into a temporary additional hall. During these alterations, the chapel screen of 1588 was discovered behind plaster of the south wall.

The early adaptations were made by Ralph Symons, who built Sidney and the Second Court of St. John's, and the college was so satisfied with his work that they leased a house to him at a low rent 'in consideracion that the said Raphe Symondes is a well mynded man towardes Emanuell Colledge in Cambridge latelie founded and newlie buylded. The workemanship whearof touching the stone worke hath been wrought and perfourmed by the said Raphe, whearin he hath shewed him selfe verie diligent and carefull'. A subway under Emmanuel Street leads to North Court, built in 1910–14.

In Front Court, the Hall, with two bay windows at the dais end, was ashlar-faced and redecorated by Essex in 1764, and he put in the delicate stucco ceiling. Beyond the Hall is the Combination Room, with a bay window of 1876. The Westmoreland Building across the court was constructed in 1719–22 to replace an earlier range. It is of three storeys, and was built by direct labour; the college nominated two Fellows to supervise the financing and construction of it. After a fire of 1811 had done much damage, it was restored to its former state. Extensive repairs have recently again been made.

To the east is Wren's Chapel with its flanking colonnades, which he designed in 1666. The proportions are not perfect, but Wren's work is the most striking in the college. There are four large pilasters supporting a frieze decorated with garlands, and a pediment with a clock in a square centre-piece, and a lantern. This is not the actual front of the Chapel, as the Master's Gallery extends along the whole width of the court. In the interior, the beautiful plaster ceiling is decorated with flowers, fruit and leaves, and the seventeenth-century woodwork was made by Cornelius Austin. Elaborately carved oak communion rails are late seventeenth century, and the cut-glass chandelier was presented in 1752. An Italian rococo painting in the reredos, The Return of the Prodigal Son, by Jacopo Amigoni, was given two years later.

In the picturesque garden, the lake was once the Friary fishpond, and the Fellows' Garden has a bath and summer-house, as at Christ's. Brick Building, at right angles to the east end of Front Court, was put up in 1633–4, a range of three storeys and attics, and it has not been much altered, although it was recently renovated. Two late nineteenth-century red brick ranges are on the far side of the Garden, and to the right a twentieth-century block, originally lecture-rooms, but later enlarged to form the new Library and reading-room. The Master's Lodge of 1873–4, described by Dr. Pevsner as 'an uncommonly ugly brick villa', was demolished in 1963.

Downing Street, opposite Emmanuel, is bordered on both sides by University scientific laboratories and museums, but we continue to follow the main thoroughfare to visit **Downing** College, which is entered through modest gates. Building commenced in 1807 on a site then still outside the town, and it was the first college to be designed on the campus plan, with its buildings disposed around a spacious lawn.

Wilkins chose a Neo-Grecian style, but unfortunately construction proceeded only slowly and his plans have been modified by later architects. By 1821 only the east and west ranges, each of four blocks, had been built, and one of these was incomplete. Towards the south, the building on the left with a portico is the Master's Lodge, and the Hall is the corresponding building to the right.

Nothing more was done until Edward Barry completed the unfinished block in 1873, and built chambers where Wilkins had intended to have screen walls. Barry also remodelled the interior of the east end of the Hall, divided it into three bays by coupled Ionic columns, with the college arms in an elaborate framing in the centre bay. In 1930–1 Sir Herbert Baker added two L-shaped ranges to the north which are inferior to those designed by Wilkins. The central range, designed by Mr. A. T. Scott, includes the apsed Chapel built in 1951–3 behind a large six-column Ionic portico. Although Wilkins' plans were altered, his buildings in the revived Greek style, placed on either side of the broad lawn, are quite unlike anything else in Cambridge, though they are perhaps too formal to be inspiring. From the grounds of Downing there is a fine view of the Roman Catholic Church of Our Lady and the English Martyrs, built in 1887–90. In Lensfield Road, the Scott Polar Research Institute is now dwarfed by the large new Chemical Laboratory.

We have completed a circular tour of the central area, but since most people who now visit Cambridge arrive by car, some interesting buildings on the outskirts, and a few more colleges, may be mentioned. From London, the boundary is reached at Trumpington, where the church possesses one of the most important brasses in England, of Sir Roger de Trumpington. On the right of the main road is the Green Man Inn, the best surviving fifteenth-century house. It is a timber-framed building, and the ground-floor hall in the centre was originally open to the roof.

The Trumpington Road passes the University Botanic Garden of 40 acres. Although it is primarily intended for teaching and research, and sends 60–70,000 specimens a year to the Botany School, the grounds and greenhouses attract many visitors. One interesting bed, 100 yards long, has plants arranged in the chronological sequence in which they were first introduced into this country. Beside the road from Newmarket is the small Sturbridge Chapel, one of the best examples of

Norman work in the county. It was originally the chapel of a leper hospital, and it is said to have been already in existence for about 75 years when it was first mentioned in 1199. The chapel probably ceased to be used for worship in the sixteenth century, and then served as a store, a drinking-booth, a barn and a stable. Sir George Gilbert Scott restored it in 1867.

From the direction of Bedford, amid attractive woodlands at the top of Madingley Hill, is the beautiful American Cemetery, with its rows of crosses and an occasional star of David on a hillside, a remarkable chapel, and a glimpse of the towers and spires of the city. The road then passes the School of Veterinary Studies, and on the left the Observatory, built by J. C. Mead in 1822–3 in a restrained Grecian style with fine stonework mouldings. A dome rises above the centre, and the wings were intended for the observer and his assistant. It was a strange architectural style to adopt for a scientific building.

Beyond the Observatory is the large site upon which **Churchill** College is being built. Here, on a cold October day, Sir Winston planted an oak and a mulberry tree, and at a lunch in King's accepted gifts of a million dollars from the Ford Foundation and £50,000 from the Transport and General Workers' Union. The arms of the college have been adapted from those of the Churchills, and the colours, chocolate and pink, are Sir Winston's racing colours. It is intended that about 70 per cent of the undergraduates will read scientific subjects, and about one-third of the members are post-graduates.

The original plans of the architect, Richard Sheppard, envisaged the main communal buildings on either side of a wide court leading from the principal entrance, and 20 small connected courts. This plan was later altered to provide nine courts, mostly of three-storeyed buildings. One critic has said that the college looks like a germ-warfare centre, and another more aptly suggested that the courts resemble cigar boxes discarded by the great man. Certainly the windowless squash court and the power-house with its factory-like chimney in the northeast corner of the site are not very attractive, and the hard and durable bricks used throughout look dull when seen from a distance, though more pleasing when closely examined. The residential courts have projecting windows with concrete beams above and below. The dominant building is the spacious Hall, 50 feet high, with a triple-barrel vaulted

39 *The former Cross Keys Inn, Magdalene Str*
(Early Sixteenth-centu

roof covered externally with copper, and glass between vertical concrete pillars in the upper half of two of the walls. Internally, two walls
are entirely covered with wood panelling of a bold ribbed design, and
the adjacent large kitchen contains a bewildering array of apparatus.
In the same block are Combination Rooms and a snack bar.

From Grange Road, the next turning to the right, there is soon a
view of the back of the University Library, then **Selwyn**, which was
still in rural surroundings when the range towards the street, designed
by Sir A. W. Blomfield in a modern Tudor style, was finished in 1882.
The same architect built the range to the north of the court and the
Chapel, completed in 1895. A Jacobean style was adopted for the
south range of 1908–9 which includes the Hall and the Combination
Room. The fine panelling of 1708 behind the dais in the Hall came from
the English Church at Rotterdam.

Sidgwick Avenue divides Selwyn from **Newnham** College, where
most of the buildings were designed by Basil Champneys. The four
earliest blocks, Old Hall (1875), Sidgwick Hall (1880), Clough Hall
(1888), containing two Combination Rooms and a Hall, and the Pfeiffer
Building (1893), are in a pleasing red brick domestic Dutch style, with
many gables and white woodwork. The traditional staircases of the
men's colleges were abandoned in favour of rooms on both sides of
corridors. A Library in a central position was built in 1897. Kennedy
Buildings (1905) and Peile Hall, facing Grange Road (1910), are in a
more restrained Neo-Georgian style. Fawcett Building, in grey brick
with broad vertical red bands, was erected along Sidgwick Avenue after
the death of Champneys in 1938, and a new gatehouse with a forecourt
in 1949. The Principal's Lodge, designed by Mr. Louis Osman, is
built around a central court in which sheets of plate glass, said to be the
largest in the world, and decorated with aluminium and coloured glass,
extend from ground to roof level. On the left side of the Avenue, a
large site is gradually being occupied by the big new buildings of Sir
Hugh Casson and Mr. Neville Conder for the Arts Faculties.

The road from Huntingdon passes **Girton** College, which is still on
the outskirts of the city. The earliest red-brick Tudor-Gothic buildings, on a spacious site of 46 acres, were opened in 1873. The architect was Alfred Waterhouse, and later buildings were designed by his
son Paul. In the early 1930s, buildings in a more attractive brick and

The yard of the Eagle Hotel, Bene't Street
The Round Church (Norman, restored in 1841)
The Principal's Lodge, Newnham College (Osman)

in a simpler style were put up by Michael Waterhouse. Nearer to the city centre, two new colleges, **Fitzwilliam House** and New Hall, are being built. The architect of the former, Denys Lasdun, has designed one block to contain the Kitchen, Hall, Combination Rooms and Library, the Hall surmounted by a very large glass 'lantern' with an undulating roof, a striking feature, especially when it is seen illuminated by night. There is a block of chambers almost parallel to the road. The dark colour of the brick used gives a somewhat austere appearance, but for **New Hall,** a white brick and precast concrete units have been chosen by the architects, Chamberlain, Powell and Bon. The first buildings are the Senior and Junior Combination Rooms, the Library, and a Dining Hall at first-floor level. The latter, presented by the Isaac Wolfson Foundation, is of a very original design, a short-armed cross surmounted by a dome and reached by four spiral staircases at the corners. To avoid the depressing effect of long corridors, the living rooms will be on staircases; in this respect the newest collegiate building adopts the traditional arrangement.

In 1963 the University Press opened a magnificent new printing house beside the railway line from London. Belatedly, in the same year, Cambridge acquired an indoor swimming pool at the corner of Mill Road, and a new fire station is being erected nearby. Lord Keynes established the Arts Theatre in 1936, but the younger inhabitants of the city still deplore the absence of an adequate dance-hall or ten-pin bowling rink, and many go to Stevenage to enjoy these amenities.

IV

The Future

ALL OF the plans for the future of Cambridge emphasise that the special characteristics of the city must be maintained. Cambridge must not be allowed to expand like Oxford, where commercial and industrial activities have irreparably harmed the atmosphere of a provincial university city. So much has been said and written about plans for Cambridge, yet since 1939 so little has been done, that one might be tempted to apply to Cambridge an observation made in 1960 by P.E.P. on Oxford planning: 'Events . . . leave the impression of a succession of plans without planning, discussions without decisions, and words without end'.

The planners confront a particularly difficult task, since a large part of the central area consists of the colleges, many with spacious grounds which limit access to the area. The road pattern cannot be much improved, because if streets such as Magdalene Street, Trinity Street and Sidney Street were to be widened, large sections of the typical physical character of the city would be destroyed. In other cities, roads can be improved and the expanding needs of commerce and business can be met by wholesale demolition and rebuilding, but this is out of the question in Cambridge. So much of the land in the centre is occupied by University or college buildings, or by groups of other property which it would be a disaster to destroy, that although the shops in the central area are now inadequate for regional needs, only minor additions can be made.

The Cambridge Development Plan was based upon recommendations made in 1950 by Sir William Holford and Professor Myles Wright. To ensure that the city would remain predominantly a University town, it was proposed that industry should be controlled so that the population within the town map area would not exceed 100,000, but development in suitable nearby villages could accommodate an additional 7,500 persons. To remedy the traffic problem, new roads and car parks were proposed. The most important of these was a 'Spine Relief Road' from the Huntingdon Road–Histon Road corner, to rejoin St. Andrew's Street at Emmanuel Street, with a New Emmanuel Road to link it with Downing Street. In the centre of the city lies the Lion Yard site now used as a surface car park. It was proposed to develop this with shops, offices and a large multi-deck car park.

The city and the University authorities accepted most of the proposals, though both doubted whether the Spine Relief Road would do all that was claimed for it. The University opposed the Lion Yard development because it would attract more traffic to the centre, and suggested that the site should be reserved for new civic buildings, including a large hall and a new public library. Cambridge lacks a large hall suitable for concerts and conferences; at present, symphony orchestras have to use the Guildhall or King's College Chapel. The University has offered to defray half of the cost of a hall.

Since the plan was made, the traffic problem becomes daily more serious. The street pattern of the historic city centre was fixed many centuries ago, when the town was little larger than a village, and when visitors arrived on horseback or in carriages. The number of people who come to Cambridge to shop or to do business, or to visit one of the finest architectural cities in the country, is constantly increasing, and the majority arrive in cars which narrow mediaeval streets and inadequate car parks cannot accommodate. Even in 1959, a survey revealed that 10,000 cars were parked in the streets in a single day. To provide for future needs, parking for at least 7,000 cars is needed. Between 1956 and 1960 the average increase in traffic and parking was 30 per cent. or 6.8 per cent. per annum compound. In 1962 the average speed in the central area was 13.5 m.p.h., and under 12 m.p.h. in some streets. And the main street through the city is in places only 15 feet 7 inches wide.

The number of people living within the town map area has been controlled, but by 1958 the unexpected increase in the birth rate had added 1,650 more inhabitants than had been forecast, and by 1971 the natural increase may be 5,700. The Development Plan assumed that a total of 187,400 for the whole county would be reached by 1971, but the 1961 census figure was 189,913, so that the estimate was exceeded 10 years sooner. Without the control of industrial development, the increase would have been even greater. The establishment of large industries of the mass-production type within the county is being discouraged, and the largest industrial concern in Cambridge, Pye Radio, was persuaded to build its mass-production factories elsewhere.

The Cambridge region attracts many research and development industries, some intimately connected with the University, which do not require much land, and many of these have been located in surrounding villages, but as more and more workers become car owners, allowing them to work where they wish, the banishment of industry to villages increases traffic. Along Victoria Avenue, traffic increased by 25 per cent. between 1956 and 1960, and in the same period the Queens' Road traffic increased by nearly 50 per cent. In the central streets the increase between 1948 and 1961 was 61 per cent.

The first review (1961) of the written statement of the Development Plan added a recognition of the importance of Cambridge as the social, cultural and commercial centre of the surrounding region. It is in the centre of the most rapidly growing area of the country, with a population increasing at more than twice the rate foreseen a decade or so ago. Cambridge is the main shopping and business centre for a large part of East Anglia, of from 300,000 to 400,000 persons. The regional functions were emphasised by the University authorities when they maintained that an increase of shopping facilities in the historic centre must be totally inadequate, and proposed that a second shopping centre should be built on an area of 65 acres bounded by Maid's Causeway, Newmarket Road, East Road, Park-side and Emmanuel Road, where there would be ample room for departmental stores and multiple shops, car parks, and adequate approach and service roads.

The County Council maintains that 'deliberately to expand the shopping and commercial activities would be contrary to the principle of the plan and would be to the ultimate detriment of the university city'. The City Council, while agreeing that shopping facilities in part of this area should be increased to relieve pressure in the centre, believes with the County that it is not desirable to dispossess a large number of householders and businesses to create a huge new shopping area. The success of the plan would entail the removal of a number of the more popular shops, and this would undoubtedly have a deadening effect on the central area and destroy the intermingling of Town and Gown. The central area is now a combination of a University and market town which Holford admired and wished to preserve. Near the ring of colleges are the multiple stores, the smaller specialist shops, banks, the Guildhall and the theatre. This historic centre must be planned primarily for pedestrians, with cars increasingly excluded. The Minister criticised the first proposals for the Lion Yard area on the ground that they would cause increased congestion, and they have since been modified to increase the retail and service space in the central area by only 8 per cent.

The Development Plan envisaged that University expansion would take place towards the west, where there is available land, and this process has already begun. Several Arts Faculties have been rehoused on the Sidgwick Avenue site, and 4,000 students will eventually use these buildings. The University believes that teaching and research in the Natural Sciences must remain within the central area. Scientific knowledge is a unity, and all scientists must be in close contact with one another. It is claimed that if the New Museums site is redeveloped to make better use of the land space, also the former site of the Pitt Press and of Addenbrooke's Hospital when the transfer to Hills Road has been completed, the Natural Sciences can remain within the centre.

The University buildings are used by 12,000 people, not only by dons and undergraduates, but by an army of laboratory and museum assistants, librarians, typists, etc. Traffic would increase if the buildings become more widely spread. The first £2 million scheme by Denys Lasdun for the redevelopment of the New Museums site aroused much criticism, particularly because it included three tall towers which would radically alter some famous Cambridge views, especially that of King's College Chapel and the Gibbs Building from the Backs.

The attempts to limit the population of the city do not have universal approval. Critics have pointed out that although the growth of industry can be controlled, commercial growth is beyond the control of the planners, since it is dependent on the wealth and mobility of those living in the area served by the city. The first Plan was made at a time of austerity and petrol rationing. Those who framed it could not foresee the rapid growth of the affluent society and the enormous expansion of car ownership. An increased population need not lead to ever-expanding suburbs. The post-war housing has been wasteful of land, and many decaying areas near the centre can be redeveloped to house more people. The University claims that nearly twice as many people could live near the centre than envisaged by the Plan. A negative policy of attempting to stabilise the total population will not attract the large investments needed for improvements. Developers and retailers are attracted to invest in expanding cities, not in those in which natural growth is being frustrated by the planning authorities.

Should a ceiling also be placed on the number of students? Many believe that the existing universities should not expand, but that a considerable number of new ones must be created. Others maintain that only very large universities can provide adequate facilities for important scientific research projects, for specialisation at professorial level, and for well-stocked libraries. Even the largest universities in this country are small compared with the 47,000 students of California, and the 20,000 or more of Illinois, Indiana or Ohio. Very big universities need large administrative staffs with systems and controls that many dons find frustrating. Similarly, there are those who ardently advocate the retention of small colleges and nostalgically recall the days when everyone in a college knew everyone else. They insist that in a small college the undergraduates gain a great deal because they can know a few learned men really well. Many of the colleges have recently built hostels far removed from the main buildings, or have taken over large houses intended for the families and servants of the nineteenth-century professors. Many assert that this policy is not in the best interests of the students, and that several new colleges would be better than any further expansion of those already in existence. Nevertheless, after the publication of the Robbins Report, a number of colleges announced that they would increase their intake of undergraduates.

There are plans for new streets and the widening of some existing thoroughfares. At present, 31 per cent of the traffic in the central area has no business in the centre, and when the street pattern has been improved, all traffic will be banned from some of the narrow streets. Traffic in Queens' Road now forms a barrier between the older colleges and University buildings and the new developments, but eventually all commercial vehicles will be banned and a speed limit of 20 m.p.h. will be imposed along the Backs. Although traffic will undoubtedly continue to increase, we may hope that by the end of the next decade at least some parts of the central area may be more peaceful than they are today.

Index of Subjects

Index

Index of People

Index

Index